Christmas 2013

ON MY WORST DAY

by John Lynch

Published by CrossSection

940 Calle Negocio #175

San Clemente, CA 92673

800-946-5983

crosssection.com

Scripture Taken from the Holy Bible, New International Version , NIV .

Copyright 1973, 1978, 1984, 2011 by Biblica, Inc.

Book + Jacket design by Crosssection

Set in Adobe Garamond & Trixie

First Edition: September 2013

Printed in the USA

ISBN 978-0-9847577-9-4 (paperback)

ISBN 978-0-9899537-0-2 (e-book)

Cheesecake, Evil, Sandy Koufax, and Jesus

I am running with everything in me. The wind coming through the ear holes in my helmet is so loud, I wonder if people in the stands can hear it. It feels like everything in my life depends upon my sliding into third base safely. Every day, something feels this important...

Today, the good guys win. I hit a triple and score the go-ahead run. And on this late spring afternoon, my team, the Upland Lions, defeat Boyd Lumber 6–3, here at Olivedale Park.

The teams shake hands, the coach talks to us for a few minutes, then everyone packs up and heads home.

... It's now two-something. I'm sitting on top of a picnic bench, in my sticky wool uniform, baking in the bright sun.

My mom is late again.

Everyone has left the stadium. The maintenance man graded the field, locked up the snack booth and has now driven off. I'm officially the last witness at the scene.

It's 1964.

I've been staring into my glove and picking mud off my cleats. I'm now trying out different sounds and voices. I'm bored. I am rarely bored. But the heat and glare are taking their toll. There's little shade yet at this recently built park.

Then suddenly, it happens. Without planning it, I find myself talking to God. I've never done it before this moment.

God, so I think you should know, I'm on to you. I know something's up. I know you're real. The other night, I was walking home in the dark. I saw things in the shadows that didn't look right. Someone was following me. I was scared. So scared. I didn't know if I should knock on a neighbor's door or start trying to outrun whoever it was until I'm home.

In that moment I called for someone I couldn't see. I whispered, "Help!" That was you. Wasn't it?

Why did I call out to you? My family doesn't believe in you. We are Unitarians, I think. I don't know what that means. But my dad says you don't exist. He says leaders made you up so people would behave better.

Anyway, I felt something I don't know how to describe. I haven't talked to anyone about it. I've never felt anything like it before. I want my whole life to be that way—the way it was those two minutes. I want it to come back so much.

So, who are you?

I see paintings and statues at churches. That can't be you. You look terrible! They make you look angry or sad or like you need some food. You have this look, like you're expecting us to do something. And nobody seems to be able to figure out what you want. And none of it matches what I felt walking home the other night.

And church people. I don't get them at all. They seem so strange to me. They're trying too hard or something. Like they're trying to convince themselves they're better than others. Maybe they are, but I would never want to be like them. Their smiles don't seem real.

Anyway, I don't know what to do next. Don't forget me. I know what I felt that night was real. I wanted you to know I know. Thanks for making the people in the bushes go away.

Then a horn honks…It's my mom, in our 1957 Chevy Biscayne.

This is the last time I will talk to him or think much about him for nearly two decades.

IIIIIIIIIIIIIIIIIIII

That boy is me, John Lynch. What follows is the chronology of figuring out how to make real the life I experienced, for several minutes, that night in the dark. My story seems to follow this progression:

- The first part of my life I spent trying to
  make myself lovable so I would be loved.
- The second part of my life I spent trying to
  make myself worthy of the love I had found.
- The third part of my life I spent trying to
  convince myself the love I had found was enough.
- This fourth part of my life I am actually beginning to
  experience the life love has given me.

So, I'm writing this book—for us. To help us believe God is daily drawing us to receive a life magnificently worthy of his love.

A life which will hold up—on my worst day.

Maybe you too will find yourself on these pages.

For he has heard your call in the dark, too… even on your worst day.

December 1958

The first Christmas gift I can remember was a rubber-tipped bow and arrow set. During the Eisenhower administration, it was maybe the finest gift available to a five-year-old. I tore into the cellophane-wrapped package and sprinted into the neighborhood to show off my six arrows and bow. I proudly carried it all in the provided plastic quiver, transported with a functional twined strap.

Our family celebrated Christmas earlier in the morning than most. So, at 7:30, I was not as welcomed into neighborhood homes as I had hoped. I was left alone to hunt imaginary weasels in my Allentown cul-de-sac.

That's when I wandered by the only manhole on our street. I had no reason to believe it wasn't the only one in the free world. One of the neighborhood kid's uncle told him if you dropped a stone into the manhole, got real quiet, and waited long enough, you could hear a person in China swear in their own language. He reasoned China was exactly across the world from us and that they didn't yet have manhole covers. Only the holes. My friends and I spent many hours around our manhole cover, to see if we could make it happen. But so far, nothing. Sitting there, now, with my bow and arrows, in front of the manhole, I began to wonder if perhaps an item with more substance would better make the journey.

This next section of this story, I still can't get my head around.

Without giving myself a chance to question my impulse, I slid one of the arrows into the tiny manhole cover hole and let it go. I listened. It made several indistinguishable sounds and then…silence. Nothing conclusive. So, I tried another. And another. Eventually, I put all my arrows down that manhole. I may have jammed the bow down there too. I had to go home without my bow-and-arrow set. The same boy who left with a bow-and-arrow set.

Later, upon questioning, I panicked and told my parents Dougie Herring had forcibly taken my arrows and put them down our manhole. He was an easy mark. Nobody liked Dougie Herring. Even his parents didn't believe Dougie's defense. That night he got the spanking of his life.

If I hadn't known by then, I knew it now. I was capable of great wrong.

I lay in bed that night wondering to myself, *What in the world happened today? Did I actually throw my entire bow and arrow set down a manhole?*

I didn't yet have anyone I could trust to talk about this, except myself. And I didn't want to talk about it. So I stuffed it. I would learn to become a very skilled stuffer over time.

I walked out my door the next morning as a kid who threw his prized possession down a manhole, and then blamed a friend for it.

Welcome to my world.

... John, you will not yet be able to hear these words, but starting today I will speak to you for the rest of your life. We can play the highlights over again when you get home. For now, they will cause you to sense something beyond your own voice when you go to bed tonight. When you finally do hear me, twenty-three years from now, you'll find it familiar enough to trust.

... So, here we go.

You are correct. Today was an odd one for you. I understand all things and I'm still not entirely certain what that was all about! The entire set of arrows? Really?

But know this: from before the world began, I wanted there to be an exact you on this planet. I picked for you to arrive into this city, Allentown, Pennsylvania. Someday, you will travel to where you were told those arrows went.

Yes, you will do bizarre stuff like this again. On a winter's day, five years from now, you will bury a brand-new sweater, which you actually like, between second and third on a local baseball field. In your forties I will have to stop you from throwing your keys overboard during a choppy ride in a friend's boat. You will reason, because you have no pockets in your swimsuit, your keys eventually will fly from your hands into the lake. Trying to avoid this tension, you will actually consider beating fate to the punch.

Even this bizarre quirk is all part of the way I created you. You'll add your own peculiar twists to it. But know this: I am never disgusted or embarrassed of who you are. Not now, not later, not ever. ... Oh, and you're going to take us to some very odd places. So, cut yourself some slack. We're just getting started on this ride. Yes, I'm aware of the lying. And I see you stuffing feelings away and going private with what confuses and embarrasses you. But yours is a book with many chapters. I'm going to need some time. ...

1960

I am sitting in my parent's 1957 green Chevy Biscayne in the Upland, California, *Shopping Bag Market* parking lot. I'm barely old enough to be left alone in the car. It's a field day for a kid to be given free rein in his parent's car! I can make so many buttons and knobs do cool things. There used to be cigarette lighters in cars. I put my finger onto the orange-hot coil. That was a mistake. I spit on my finger and keep working my way around the dash. I run the wiper blades. I spin the dial across the radio. I honk the horn, making shoppers jump as they carry groceries past our car. I must be the funniest boy in town!

After awhile it dawns on me, my parents have been inside the store a long time. Uncomfortably long. *What could take so long in a grocery store? You buy your stuff and check out. It's not like there's a theater in there!* I fiddle awhile longer with mirrors and seat adjustments. Still no parents. Then this: *What if they're so sick of being my parents, they've planned this opportunity to slip out the back? They're willing to give up the car and their home and spend the rest of their lives on the run, if they can get away from me.* I'm seven, maybe eight; and in this moment, this is the most logical, reasonable explanation I can come up with.

Where does that come from?

My parents love me. On occasion they tell me. They feed me and wash my clothes. They signed me up for school and take me to Dodger games. But my best explanation for them being too long in a grocery store was child abandonment. I am strategizing my next few hours as an orphan when they walk out. I realize now how deeply this runs in my DNA. Nothing really sad, no traumatic rejection has yet happened to me. No relatives have died. I don't like girls yet. But this internal voice plays, without sleep: *Something about you John, is fundamentally wrong. Given enough time, people will reject you. Others aren't like you. They are normal and worth loving. Apparently, you are neither. Figure out some reason to be loved; some talent to keep people around, or this is going to be a very lonely and hard life.*

In a hundred different ways I can still create scenarios of impending abandonment. Now it's my wife, or those closest to me.

I wonder if all of us, early on, experience something similar. Some go my route. Others pretend they are superior and everyone else is suspect. Either way, we're all bluffing, whistling in the dark, until something or someone comes to convince us of our actual worth.

1962

I'm still not sure where we got the idea to hammer ordinary rocks from our backyard into pieces, put them into a shoebox, and then sell them to our neighbors. We thought our yard was different from other yards. Ours apparently had magic rocks. Why else would neighbors give us money for them?

We'd simply knock on a neighbor's door and confidently say, "Hey, look at these. Would you like to buy any?"

"You're Jim and Pat Lynch's kids, aren't you?"

"Why, yes we are!"

This would be usually followed by an awkward silence ... then a call into the house, for help. "Margaret! Do we want any broken rocks from the Lynch's backyard?"

Eventually the man at the door would look into the shoe box, scratch around with his finger, and mumble, "Oh, I guess I'll take this one. How much?"

"A dollar."

I'm pretty sure we pulled down thirty bucks that first day. There was growing concern we'd soon run out of magic rocks in our yard.

I remember telling my dad about the rock sales and that I was willing to help him out financially. He got very upset with us. I didn't understand. Maybe someone was a bit jealous his children were making almost as much as him!

Several years later, Dave Barrows and I often didn't have enough spare money for candy and snacks after school. So we started doing scavenger hunts. An older group of kids had knocked on our door the weekend before and recited to my mom a long list of unusual items. I watched my mom eagerly come back with several of the objects from the list. She was so happy to do so. I thought to myself in that moment: *This is too easy.*

The following Monday, Barrows and I hit the neighborhoods. Every time out it was the same. "Hello ma'am. I'm John Lynch; this is Dave Barrows, and we're team blue on a scavenger hunt for our youth group. We're hoping you might have one of these following items. An Egyptian peacock feather, a bronzed bust of Abraham Lincoln, a picture frame made from gun powder ... and a nickel from between 1950 and 1960."

"Hmmm. Well boys, let me go take a look." She'd come back saying, "I honestly thought we might have that bronzed Lincoln. ... But here's a nickel from 1957. Does this help?"

I never thought we were being bad. I saw it like Halloween. You do your part, do the work, be cute, and neighbors give you stuff.

I have a feeling this conversation went on in heaven that night, between God and the angels:

I like the kid. I really do. But he does some of the oddest things, doesn't he? Still, he's got to gain some confidence and learn to tell stories. Don't forget, when he's in college, he'll spend an entire summer walking door to door, unsuccessfully trying to sell Fuller Brushes. So, I say, let the boy have some coins for an Abba-Zaba.

1962

Our principal at Baldy View Elementary walks into my fourth-grade class like she's about to announce one of our students has landed on the moon. She calls Susan Sato up front. "Students, several weeks ago Susan turned this quarter into the office. She found it on the playground and wanted to make sure it got to the person who lost it. We waited to see if anyone would come looking for it. Today, I return this quarter to you, Susan, with great appreciation for your honesty." The whole room applauded like she'd been awarded the medal of distinguished service. She was like a hero at our school for the next few weeks. Kids would ask to see the famous quarter.

That evening I took a five-dollar bill from my mom's wallet. I didn't think she'd notice and I'd have it back to her soon enough, along with some world-class praise and attention for her son.

I turned in the bill to the office. "I found this out on the playground. I was going to take it home but I thought someone might miss it if it was theirs."

The lady at the front desk was not impressed. She appeared inconvenienced.

Wait, I'm thinking, *where's the principal?*

I wanted to ask for the money back and come back at a more strategic time. "How long before, well, we know if someone claims it?"

She was vague. "If the principal comes to your class, you'll know."

"So, you'll be sure to keep it safe and stuff, um, in case someone wanted to claim it?" She shrugged more than nodded.

I waited … And waited … And waited. Every day for five weeks I prepared myself for the principal's arrival to my classroom. Imagine, if a quarter got such a response, what five dollars would get me!

The principal never came.

Finally, I went to the office and asked, "So, I turned in a five-dollar bill awhile ago. I was just wondering when the principal will be coming to our class."

The same lady at the front desk looked at me coldly. "Oh. Someone claimed that. Thanks."

I was devastated. I wanted to yell out, "Hey, lady, that was *my* money! The only person who could claim it to be lost was *me*. And the only one who knew about it was you. You took my money, you old hag!"

But I knew she had me. If she told the principal I brought my own money in to get back and be awarded for, I'd be in big trouble.

I walked backwards out of the office, glaring at her. She held eye contact with a forced smile which said, "I've already spent your money, you little chump."

Two lessons emerged from the experience. First, I realized adults in roles of authority do not always have your best interest at heart.

And I freshly discovered the lengths I would go to be adored and praised. I never told my mom. I only learned to bury deeper the truth of what I was capable of doing.

John, I know what happens from here. You will want to dig yourself deeper into shame. You stole money from your mom, and then lost what belonged to her to a dishonest person. You took from your parents so you could get from your friends.

… I get it. I watched it. But this is not the whole story. I've built into you a longing to have your life count, to be affirmed for giving away what I've given you. You just don't know how to do it yet. In your immaturity, this looked like a quick way to fill that longing. You will walk down tens of dozens of blind alleys before you are convinced none of these false attempts will give you what you're looking for. Even if the principal had given you the money, it wouldn't have paid off. I've built life that way. You can get everything, climbing to the top of the heap, but I will always be the only one who can couple the experience with joy.

I will direct your parents to buy a few acres of land in a few years, which will more than compensate for what you lost. It wouldn't hurt you to voluntarily do something around the house. It might make you feel better until you understand how forgiveness and repentance work.

I do have to say, you had a very creative plan. Some kids might think to do it, but you actually tried it! It was terribly flawed. But had that front desk lady been honest you might have pulled it off. Nothing's changed between us. I saw this one coming for a long time.

So, here I am, already fully locked into this reality: **"The first part of my life I spent trying to make myself lovable so I would be loved."**

1962

Mr. Yukech passed away from kidney failure this year. He lived across the street, on Altura Way. For some reason, he took a kind interest in me. If he saw me playing out front, he'd usually walk over. We'd sit for hours on our front stoop. Who does that? A sixty-some-year-old and a kid spending unhurried chunks of time together. I felt known with him, even not talking at all. I think, all along, he was trying to convince me I was worth his time. Like that single gift would help me.

He had no idea how much it would.

He talked to me about life, about nearly everything. He was wise. I listened to him, because even then I could tell he wasn't giving adult slogans. He listened to me, like what I was saying was important. He was real. Most adults saw me as a disrespectful, spoiled punk. So did Mr. Yukech. But he was able to see over it all. He gave me my first baseball glove. He restrung one from his garage and rubbed saddle soap into every crevice. I'd give up a lot to have that glove today.

During my entire childhood, he was the only adult I visited in a hospital. I made my parents drive me there. When he ultimately passed away from kidney failure, it was the first time I'd experienced deep loss.

When I eventually did start to risk trusting others, it was largely because I'd once known someone trustworthy. I would waste far too much of my life in foolishness, without wisdom, fighting *this* truth:

Awakening: *Anyone can get knowledge and information; but nobody gets wisdom, insight, and discernment without trusting.*

Ever since Mr. Yukech, I was looking hard for such a place.

John, I will make sure Bill Yukech sees this piece.

1962

I have never known anyone with a more beautiful heart than my mom. She was a language teacher and a linguist. At the time of her death, she was writing a book on root similarities of the romance languages. She sang opera professionally. She was the kindest, most other-centered person I have ever met.

I was always told both my parents were atheists. But I have this memory. It still makes me cry. One evening my dad and I got into an argument over something. I was sent to my room—livid, shaking, fighting back tears until I got out of his presence. Later, my mom knocked on the door of my room, entered, and sat next to me on my bed. She stroked my hair and eventually whispered "John, there's a place coming where there are no tears and the real you will be fully known. There is one who will make sense of all the pain. I promise you."

It was unlike anything she'd ever said to me. We never spoke of it again. I never knew what to do with it. I've wondered if those words guided me to him. I picture her in heaven.

John, sometimes people trust me early on and then their lives gets misdirected. They marry someone who doesn't trust me. Or the melody gets lost amid pain. But I don't forget. No matter how faint, distorted or convoluted, I can ferret out trust. I gave you an astoundingly good mother. You did not yet know how to return her love. You were a kid. But she knows now. I want you to know that. I've not forgotten and she knows. That's as far as we can go right now. Her words set you on a journey for the land and person she described. You will be twenty-five when she leaves this world. You will lay sprawled out on a boulder in the middle of a Connecticut forest, crying out to whoever holds forever. You will beg and demand and shout to be assured she is safe. You will ache for there to be a God– a good and real and powerful God. You will tell me what she said that evening on your bed ... John, I missed not one word. I was there, on the boulder with you. And I do only right.

February 9, 1964

This evening, the Beatles, in their first visit to America, appeared on the Ed Sullivan show; 728 people witnessed the event in Studio 50. Seventy-four million of us stared at it on television. Most of us will never be the same. I sat there, transfixed, as though watching a talent show from another galaxy. The next morning, at school, no one greeted each other without the next sentence containing the words "the Beatles."

For me it was so much more than the excitement of a once-a-century phenomenon. It was my indelible introduction into a lifelong obsession with becoming famous.

I soon bought a Beatles wig and was singing "It Won't Be Long" into the stereo speakers in our den—imagining I was lead singer and rhythm guitarist in a band which would eventually eclipse the popularity of the Beatles.

I usually pictured in the audience my teachers and all those who did not understand or appreciate me. Now they were leaning over to each other between songs, confessing, "I was wrong. This young man is so incredible. I always knew it, really."

So, there you go. It's not the Beatles' fault. It was in me before they showed up. For a long time I would feel the need to prove a worth which matched my need to be loved.

It's a chump's bet, a longing that can never pay off. Even if people get it, they then wish they didn't have it. As Steve Martin writes, "I was once not enough famous. Then I was too famous. Now I'm just right famous."

Even today, I can't defend my motives at any given time. I used to rough myself up for not having more "godly" ambitions. I was fairly certain he couldn't use me if my motives weren't almost completely right.

Anymore though, I imagine him saying something like this:

John, your motives will always be less than pure. I'm actually good with that. Maturity takes a lifetime. If I had to wait for humans to get their motives 80 percent right before I could work with them, soup wouldn't have yet been invented! You know what will one day change? You. Your entire wiring. Yes, you will still sometimes want to be adored by all mankind. But you will find yourself increasingly more concerned about others, about destiny about having this life count. Don't be hard on yourself. You're right on time. ...

1964

As a boy, I remember thinking there was nothing as stupid or irrelevant as anything having to do with God. The Lynches were atheists. Dad progressively pushed to get us away from celebrating Christmas. His ultimate act was to have us open gifts the evening before. (Way to stick it to the man, Dad!) He brought home an aluminum tree in 1957 and we put it up every year through the late '70s, after over a third of the limbs no longer had tinsel. Most of our few ornaments eventually slid to the center. Other kids had sprawling, flocked trees with color wheels, popcorn, cranberries, and shiny ornaments, all animated by the warmth of nearly endless strands of lights. The Lynches had sticks shoved into a pole, covered with shredded aluminum foil. I tried to not have friends over during December. Dad made sure we received mostly educational gifts or underwear, so we wouldn't get enthralled with the holiday. Nothing says Christmas like unwrapping a bag of thin dress socks.

As a kid, every picture or statue I saw of Jesus depressed or spooked me. His eyes followed me, like he was trying to get my attention so he could tell me off. "Hey, you, kid. Yeah, you. Look over here at me! Wipe that grin off your face. I'm carrying the weight of the world, and you couldn't care less … I didn't come to earth for you."

I was never supposed to get Jesus. I was sure God was, as Karl Marx had said, "the opiate of the masses." Everything about me cried out against everything to do with God.

Except this thought I couldn't turn off …

Awakening: *No matter how diligently parents try to train a child in the absurdity of faith in God, they can't stop his voice: "What if I'm here, after all? What if I think about you every moment of the day? What if I hold that magic your heart keeps waiting to be true?"*

It followed me at night, on walks home. It stayed with me through the years when I mocked his name. I lived my entire childhood claiming to not believe in a God I secretly wanted.

1964

You couldn't walk any significant distance in my childhood Upland without going through an orange grove. In the winter, the owners kept the fruit from freezing at night through a series of oil-generated, heat-producing "smudge pots." The ignited oil in those squatty metal drums placed along the rows of trees gave off a dirty, smoky warmth. The orchard formed a warm canopy and temporary home for drifters or those hiding from local authorities. What a different time it was in the world! My friends and I were always fascinated, getting to hang out with real hobos. We'd stand around them, speechless, like we were watching men from another planet.

I especially remember one in particular. He had thick oily hair, wore a flannel shirt and greasy jeans. He looked pretty beaten down. But he seemed so cool, living alone out under the sky. He was sketchy looking—pretty quiet and wearing a nervous tic. But he was kind, careful to not frighten us with the gruff realities of his journey. He showed us how to cook things with aluminum foil on an open fire. He'd grill up corn, pancakes, and pieces of what he called "sparrow meat." He sometimes whittled while he talked to us. We never once thought about any danger.

Today, imagine a kid telling his mom, "Hey, I'm going with my friends to visit a vagrant out in the orange groves. He has a knife."

It all set a course for me. It caused me to not fear those on the edges of society. Years later I discovered the ones who talk to me most genuinely, tenderly, and authentically about God are often those having the toughest time managing daily life in society. Somehow, they manage to most clearly see God in the midst of it.

This childhood freedom would teach me to give dignity with my time, attention, and presence to those who doubt their life matters. To those whose failure and weaknesses try to convince them they are a different class of human. Great beauty doesn't avoid the most poor, fragile, or devastated. Sometimes dignity is giving importance to those who sit on the fringe. It is convincing them God loves them as well as anyone else. I think it's why I love *Cannery Row* so much. Steinbeck gave dignity to those who have no visible footing in this world. I have discovered most of my favorite speaking events have been to the painfully common, limping, and inappropriate. More often than not, they enjoy my humor the most, listen most intently to my words, and lavish me with the most pie. Maybe it's all because, behind my loud and articulate bluster, I am one of them.

I imagine that evening Jesus took Levi, the hated tax-gatherer, up on his invitation to dinner. A roomful of actively immoral outcasts, carrying all manner of visible scars of depravity, desperately trying to be on their best behavior. Quiet and awkward. If we could have filmed it, the camera would now pan in from above, through the room to where Jesus is reclining. ... Soon there's a circle around Jesus, all of them gradually sitting up, elbows on knees, chins on hands. Hardened sinners with expressions of wonder and innocence. We're watching what happens when perfect love, grace, and purity invade darkness. The King has shown up to rescue prisoners from the enemy camp—where wickedness and perversion have seemed logical up until this moment. Suddenly there is, at least in this room, a hope life could be different.

The night air gradually blends into a mixture of the best humor, stories, truth, life, hope. Somewhere in the evening, the conversation turns.

"Who are you—really?" He unhurriedly lets them ask questions. Then there is silence. It is becoming clear exactly who he is. Few in the crowds outside, who've sought him for a miracle show, receive what these reprobates are receiving. They're becoming desperate for who he is, not what magic he might wave.

Someone sitting next to him: "Why us? Why would you choose to be here tonight, with us?"

Jesus: "This may be hard for you to understand. I've known you and loved you since before there was time. I've watched it all. I know about the catch in your knee that takes until after noon to loosen up. I was there the evenings your father beat you. I was there when you were kicked out of the synagogue. And now, I've come from heaven for you."

"But ... don't you know what I've done?"

"Yes, I do. And I have the unfortunate ability to know the wrong things you're going to do tomorrow and the day after that. The only sin which could possibly separate you from eternity with God is to reject the person who's speaking to you at this moment." ... He smiles. "And, I gotta tell you, I'm being welcomed here tonight like few other places since I've been down here. ... Now, may I finish this joke?"

... And two dozen men and women, who walked into this party ready for a fight, laugh deeply ... and peer into his eyes, like convicts about to receive their walking papers.

1964

Few foods captivated me in youth like cheesecake. I was always left frustrated, wanting more than I was allowed in any given sitting. My parents never allowed it into our home, treating cheesecake as a luxury only royalty should possess—like caviar or gold-leafed chocolate dishes. On the rare occasion Dad did take us to a restaurant that might carry cheesecake, he'd always made sure he pointed out the ridiculously high price of desserts. Reading the menu, he'd grumble under his breath, "These desserts cost about what I make in a day's work. What sort of people would order such a thing?"

But on my birthday last year he took us to the Magic Lamp—the nicest restaurant in Upland. It had white linen tablecloths and bread sticks in a basket covered with a matching linen napkin. My dad allowed me to order dessert!

When it finally arrived, it was so incredibly thin and tiny. A sliver of cheesecake, nearly lost on the dessert plate. The waiter could have served it with tweezers. I'm thinking, "I could down about nineteen of these!"

When I asked if I could have a second piece, my dad looked at me like he might give his speech about people starving in the Congo.

… All of this is to help explain to you why this summer day in 1964 turned out the way it did.

I was pedaling my blue Sting-Ray into downtown Upland to watch a matinee at the Grove

Theater. I didn't make it that far. Turning off Euclid onto Ninth Street, I was physically pulled by what smelled like freshly baked cheesecake. The aroma came from the Upland Bakery. I was suddenly positioned in front of the glass store window in time to watch an oversized man in a white baker's uniform slide a majestic, freshly baked cheesecake from an oven with a immense wooden paddle.

(I am oft and accurately accused of runaway hyperbole, but none of what I am about to write bears the marks of such device.)

I walked into the store and up to the glass counter, on whose racks the cake had only now been placed. Pointing to it, while making eye contact with the woman behind the counter, I asked, "How much for this. How much does it cost?"

"Per slice?"

"No. The whole cheesecake. How much?"

She quoted a nearly impossible amount. But I would find a way to purchase this. The thought that I could, for once, have all the cheesecake I wanted had suddenly become the single most important goal for this day of my life.

I spoke out, clearly and slowly, "Would you please not let anyone else buy this? I'm going to go home to find the money to buy it. Promise?"

And I was off on my bicycle.

Mom was not home. I had eighty-five cents already on me for the movie and snacks. I dug through my dad's change cup in his dresser. I scoured every room of the house. I probably rounded up a dollar's worth of coins—still pitifully short of the amount to own that cake.

… Then I remembered my Indian Head nickel collection.

A child of the depression, my dad now had many collections—perhaps as a hedge against impending poverty. He wanted me to have a similar passion. So he had purchased a fleet of these heavy cardboard blue booklets with slots for Indian Head nickels. A slot for every year they were minted. Dad helped me get started with some fairly rare coins. I soon got into it, and in the last several years had filled many of the slots.

Somehow able to ignore perspective, consequence, and future regret, I bent back the cardboard booklets and popped out coins—until I had over five dollars worth of nickels in the pockets of my jeans. I got back on my Stingray and raced to the bakery. There, I proceeded to pour out piles of nickels onto that counter.

I walked out with the entire cheesecake in a box!

I should have taken the cake home and shared half with my family. I did not do that.

I should have located a plastic fork and knife and eaten it at a local park. I did not do that.

I should have at least sat down. I did not do that.

I walked into the alley behind their store. Like a child raised by wolverines, I began breaking off huge chunks of warm, fresh cheesecake and shoving them into my mouth. It tasted so incredibly good.

For almost minutes.

To my credit, I was over halfway through the giant cake before it became oppressive. I was now slowly and reluctantly wadding it into my mouth. I started feeling sick two-thirds of the way through … and tossed the rest in a dumpster several feet away.

I wandered around to the front, a boy dazed by sugar and disappointment. *What just happened?* I thought, as I stared at the road, slowly weaving my bike through the neighborhoods toward home. *What will I tell Dad about the nickels? Someday he's going to want to see how the collection is going. Why did I do that? What is wrong with me?*

But, later that evening, an even deeper question worked its way to the surface: *Why didn't that work today? Why didn't that cheesecake make me happier?*

I don't think either of my parents ever heard this story. I can't remember how I explained the missing nickels. But I walked forward from that day, on a more urgent mission—to find what food, entertainment, activity, or repetition of activity would satisfy me long enough to satisfy this unmet urge inside me.

John, I do not want to rub this in; but if you'd held onto those Indian head nickels, you could buy everyone in Upland a cheesecake ... once a month ... for the rest of their lives.

Trying to solve this internal craving will be the singular driving force for decades of your life. It will harm you more than any person can. It will break your heart. One day, no time soon, you will find what your longing and unmet urges are calling for. Then, you will begin to learn what gives food its maximum taste, experiences their full measure of joy, and sunsets their full beauty. I'm right here. Though you will go into some very strange places, this obsession will not destroy you. One day, your willingness to articulate your battle with it will make you safe and real and trusted to others. Until that time, you will crave the Jack in the Box taco combo like few things on earth. I'd say you could do worse, but I'm not sure I'd be accurate. ...

1964

These days I care mostly about running fast, listening to Vin Scully describe the Dodgers on the radio and convincing enchanting Lucille Engle to like me. Orange trees still outnumber homes. Life is pretty idyllic.

Except my fifth-grade class is run by this tough kid.

He has two older brothers who, for all I know, are already in prison. Or should be. I don't yet know much about evil; but his family is evil. Donald has beaten up three kids in our class … and it's only October. He doesn't hit me because he's entertained by me.

One day he informs me we are to meet at the railroad tracks this coming Saturday morning. These particular tracks run through the center of town, ending at an orange-packing plant. For us kids, that plant is a glorious place. Upland is one of the great citrus hubs. Dozens of open-topped freight cars are three-quarters filled with oranges, waiting to be sent out to places like Billings or Topeka. On late afternoons, after cul-de-sac Wiffle ball or front-yard football, dozens of us could be found lying on our backs inside train cars filled with huge, nearly fluorescent oranges. The workers didn't even care we were in there. There were so many oranges. We'd eat them until our mouths burned. Nobody had scurvy in our neighborhood.

On this day, like six-dozen times before, I climb the train's steel ladder and dive into orange heaven. But it's early Saturday morning. No one else is yet in the cars. Donald follows me in. He leans slowly against the back wall, saying nothing. He's staring at me, intensely. I am experiencing the sensation of being trapped for the first time in my life.

He slowly informs me what he will now do to me, and what I will now do to him—twisted perversion I've never before heard or thought of.

… That morning changes my life. I remember little of what happened after emerging from that boxcar: how I got home, or what I did when I got there. I have no memories of Donald after that morning. I do carry this embedded maxim, which has clung to me like a wet sweater all my life:

"No one must ever know what happened. I will go this alone. I must find a way to never think about this again. I will be all right. I will be all right. …"

And a previously innocent and playful kid walks with a limp from that thought on.

I'm still funny. I still seem like a normal kid. I will pitch on my town's Little League All-Star team. Lucille Engle will like me. But something insidious is going on inside. All alone. Inside.

I've discovered since, there is a word for this silent limp:
Shame.

Awakening: *Guilt says I've done something wrong. Shame hisses there's something uniquely, irrevocably and fundamentally wrong with me.*

Shame tries to convince us that we caused the evil which happened to us. It continually whispers if anyone could know the truth about who we are, they would leave or pity us. So we are left to bluff and posture, guard and defend. Shame teaches us to perform for God's acceptance, to keep paying for something we eventually can no longer even name.

It will take forty years before I risk even a hint to anyone that something happened back there.

The boxcars still stand. Rusting and silent. A visible and definable part of Upland's past. My past. I've driven past them dozens of times, bringing my family to see the town of my childhood. No one in our car ever noticed me staring at those boxcars as we drove by.

Decades after that day in the boxcar, I cling to this:

Jesus, you make no mistakes; you make even better beauty out of the most heinous. You never left my side. You hated it more than I did. You give me dignity. You continue to stand with me in the arena to protect my heart and reputation. You are redeeming and will redeem all this damage. You died to take away the power of this shame. Jesus, you dropped everything to stand over me the day it all turned dark. ...

1964

Christmas is the best holiday for kids. Hands down.

... But Halloween is the coolest.

In my childhood, all the kids wore their costumes to school. All day! And there was no political rightness to navigate. Nearly every ethnicity and station in society was represented and welcomed. Indian chiefs, ghosts, angels, and Vikings played kickball next to minstrels, Moses, belly dancers, sombrero-wearing Spaniards, and hobos.

That year I went as the devil.

Imagine my mom at Coronet's department store, sorting through all the costumes: cowboys, doctors, astronauts. "Hmmm. Look at this. The devil. Yes, I think that's the most fitting outfit for my son. I'll get him the devil costume."

... I was so proud of her.

Trick or Treat in the '60s was so different than today's sanitized "Tribute to Harvest," or whatever it has become. Our own neighbors created haunted houses, with all manner of horrifying dramatics, designed solely to horrify children. A snarling, snapping German Shepherd might meet us at the door—within feet of us. On a leash, but still showing his teeth. Strangers would leap out of bushes with real axes or shovels in their hands, shouting at us. Then they'd laugh and hide back in the bushes for the next wave of kids. Unexplained explosions and shrieking filled the night air. No wonder my generation ends up in more counseling than any preceding it. ...

Old Mr. Dobbs, three houses up our street, was a Halloween legend. An odd, grumpy recluse who on Halloween night came to life. He positioned dry ice and cobwebs all over his compound. You could hear his eerie music and sound effects blocks away. His entire family would dress in black—each with a singular goal of scaring the pee out of children. One might jump from the roof, squirt fake blood on us from a missing arm, and then run off. Or from under a car, one would suddenly grab my foot as I walked up the driveway.

Each year Dobbs made "eyeball soup." We were certain that neighborhood cats were unwillingly involved in his recipe. ... I still am.

Parents didn't walk with us after, say, age six. Packs of us would roam the neighborhoods; pillowcases in hand, wearing outfits with plastic masks which caused us to keep breathing our own air.

Total strangers gave us candy! Big time candy. We might be handed two full-sized Snicker bars, without a blink.

But the best part of the whole evening was afterwards. I'd haul my candy into my room, close the door, and begin the sacred candy sorting ritual. I didn't know anyone who didn't do it. There were the "A" candies: Snickers, Butterfingers, Baby Ruth bars, etc. "B" candies included Big Hunk, Mike and Ike, and the rest of that ilk. Gum, lollipops, Boston Baked Beans and such made up the "C" category. And then there were the wretched "D" candies: candy corn and those Styrofoamlike Circus Peanuts, with colors not found in nature.

I'd lay them all out in rows of merit and then stand back to admire my evening's effort.

… The next day, arriving home from school, most of rows "A" and "B" and some of row "C" were gone.

Gone. Not there. Vanished.

I first blamed my brother. I even blamed my parents. It was a mystery which drug on for months.

Until my dad's mother passed away.

She lived her last several years with us. She and I were not especially close. Living in our den, she mostly only came out at meal time. She was in her late eighties, which at that time was like being in her late one-hundred-twenties.

One afternoon, as my parents were packing up her belongings, my mom called me into the den. "John, come look at this." And there, in the top drawer of her desk, were the wrappers and remaining pieces of uneaten candy. My candy.

My grandmother had shuffled into my bedroom when no one was around and filled her spindly, saggy little arms with my candy. She probably had to make several trips. I'm not certain I've forgiven her yet.

Somehow, I wound up with her Bible. She had underlined verses and wrote the date next to them. Some of the citations were from back as far as the 1880s. I'd think to myself, "Wow,

there wasn't electric lighting yet. She'd have to read her Bible with a kerosene lamp!" Until one day someone mentioned in passing, "Or, maybe she read it during the day."

"Ah, yes. Perhaps she read it during the day. Certainly a viable option …"

John, I recently asked your grandmother if she ever regretted taking your candy. These are her exact words: "No. Not once. He was an annoying child. And I do so love the chocolates. No, I have no regrets."

1965

I won the fifty-yard dash two years in a row at Camp Oaks, up near Big Bear
Lake. I still have the ribbons somewhere in my attic. No one had ever won two
years in a row. And probably no one had ever made themselves more sickly nervous before a race. The rest of the kids ran because it was fun, or because they
thought they had a chance to win. I ran it knowing anything but a win would
be tragic. It was what I did, what I was known for. Winning that ribbon would
prove for another day that I was enough. Winning it would cause me to be valued and popular. There was no other option. At that age, I thought I might be
the fastest boy in my age group, anywhere. My "anywhere" was the size of Camp
Oaks and the two hundred some campers on site during my week.

Looking back, none of my friends were there. Most of the camp kids I never
saw again. My parents thought it would be a good idea to send me to a camp.
When I got home, I proudly displayed my ribbon on the living room table. My
parents both nodded and smiled politely. But it wasn't that "Oh my gosh, you're
amazing!" kind of response. Dad said something like, "See, son? That's why we
send you to camp. Everyone gets to win at something."

So who was I running for? I didn't enjoy a thing about the race itself. I hated
the nervousness I felt for hours before it. The pushing and shoving directly before the gun sounded was chaotic and ugly. Intimidating bigger kids shuffled the
weaker and smaller behind them. The race itself
was only terror—two hundred screaming kids, all clawing out of the gate
to take away my destiny. The honor after the race was almost nonexistent. Moments after ours, another race started, followed by another. By dinner, most of
the day had blurred into one long camper decathlon.

Few seemed to even remember I'd won.

It shouldn't work like that. Greatness should be rewarded. Greatness should
result in happiness. I'm sure many of the "average" kids thought I was living the
dream. Turns out we were all kidding ourselves. We were all fighting our own
story of insecurity. And insecurity is not solved by achievement. Insecurity is
not solved by not worrying about achievement. Insecurity, it turns out, is solved
only by believing the truth about how you're seen by the only one whose opinion
ultimately matters. … And he and I were not yet talking.

That evening, lying in my bunk, arms folded behind my head, I felt very
alone in the world.

I wish you could hear me tonight. I will watch you repeat this cycle too many hundreds of times. I wish you could have seen what I saw today. You were magnificent! You blew everyone away and kept pulling further ahead. But you keep missing it. You're already worried about the next race before you receive the ribbon for this one. So soon, you'll be older and your knees will hurt. You'll be too heavy to want to sprint from place to place. I made you with this gift to enjoy, now. And you're missing it.

One day you will let me in. You will discover I do not ascribe to the false story of your unacceptability. Your proving and grinding will be gradually replaced with contentment, as you begin to let me achieve great good in you for others' benefit. That day is coming. In the meantime, though no one noticed or cared enough today, I did. I'll show you the tape when you get home. I've already showed it around here a number of times. Now go to sleep, my friend. That's another thing you won't be able to do as well when you get older.

1965

When my parents hurt my feelings, the biggest threat I could drum up was that I might run away.

One day I told them I was going to run away. Now I had to now actually do it, for at least an afternoon, or I'd forever lose the only real leverage a kid has.

My dad, calling my bluff, gathered up some items, saying, "Here, let me help."

I packed some sandwiches, another shirt, and a jacket into a grocery bag and walked out the front door, into my future.

They let me walk out! They said goodbye like I was heading across the street to a friend's house. There were no cell phones back then. They had no way of calling me to beg me back.

I made it as far as the Red Hill Bowling Lanes, four miles away. I spent the afternoon watching people bowl, eating my sandwiches, sitting in the booths above the lanes. It doesn't take long watching bad bowlers to arrive at the conclusion life on the road might be a bit overrated.

I returned home six hours later. They were out shopping. When they did eventually come home, they acted like nothing had happened. We never talked about it. We just sort of went on. ... So much for leverage.

As I grew into a teenager, I began to imagine the day when I would run away. They would deeply regret their capricious use of authority.

I never did it. But over time, the concept itself has become my default button. Only now, nearly fifty years later, my bags are a little bit more sophisticated. But they are packed. You might not know it to look at me. I've owned the same home for a quarter century. But almost every day I envision an "out." You get revealed if you stay in a community long enough. And the community gets revealed too. We can begin to imagine life somewhere else is much better.

It's all in my head, where you can't see it.

Maybe I'd go to a beach town. I'd be on a friendly, chatty, waving relationship with dozens of the locals. Stacey and I would know several couples fairly well. But this time I'd play it closer to the vest. I wouldn't dream nearly so much, risk so much, reveal so much. I'd be known as someone who once did something. But no one would know enough to have my weaknesses revealed.

Awakening: *The only one I cannot protect is myself. I must trust the commitment of another.*

I'm not sure I'll ever be free of packed bags. I'm not sure it's even the point. Grace anticipates mess and ongoing imperfection. If my needs went away, I would never experience the love of others. So, I will always carry junk, unresolved sludge, weakness, failure; things that go bump in the night.

Love eventually finds people who will not let us put our bags into the car. Who will love us for who we are, not who we can present on our best day. It's a scary risk. It gives something and takes something away. It gives us a place. But it demands us to have a better reason than shame or fear to leave to a place which is not our home.

1966

Among my six favorite days on this planet is the one Dave Barrows and I spent in the summer of 1966. We decided to hitchhike from our home to Dodger Stadium in L.A. We never thought twice of any danger. I mean, we were nearly fourteen! I have no memory of how we got there, but vivid, Technicolor memory of nearly every moment once inside the stadium. The Dodgers were playing the Giants in a doubleheader. One price, two games. Three times the magic!

What we could afford was up in the top row of the stadium. When we finally made our way to our seats, neither of us spoke for a while. We were out of breath and deeply disappointed. Far below, the players looked like ants in uniforms.

Several minutes into trying to convince ourselves these seats would work, we decided to take a huge gamble. We had no game plan. But we would find a way down into the bottom section. The stadium was packed but we had to try. Even if we could only watch close up for an inning or two, it would be worth spending the rest of the day in a basement office with security guards.

We eventually conned our way down to the entrance of the bottom level. We didn't see anyone asking for tickets so we started our way down toward seats our own parents could never afford.

I think we might have made it. Except this kindly looking older man, wearing a Dodger-blue straw hat called out, "Gentlemen, excuse me. One moment."

We made the mistake of looking back.

He gestured us toward where he was standing. "May I see your tickets, please?"

"Well, um. You see, our parents are down there and …" Dave took over. "They've got our tickets. We told them we'd be right back."

"Gentlemen, may I see your tickets?"

We each pulled out our tickets, knowing our dream was over.

He looked at them. Then he looked at us. Then he leaned his head way back, up to where our seats were. Then he looked back at the tickets. Then he looked at us again. He made a sucking sound older people make with their teeth and lips when they're considering something. He mumbled to himself. Then, very seriously he spoke, "Follow me." We did. He walked us down into the great bowl: past the wealthy people, past the players' wives, past the scouts, past the owners … all the way down to directly behind the third base dugout. The Dodger's dugout! Without smiling, he looked at our tickets and then at us, saying clearly and loudly, "Gentlemen, I believe these are your seats."

By the time we sat down, stared, and realized what had happened, we turned and he was gone.

We watched a double header from where God sits when he watches the Dodgers play.

Koufax pitched one of the games. Sandy freaking Koufax! Maury Wills stole a base. Willie Davis dove to make a one-handed catch in center. We bought Dodger dogs and frozen malts. It was a bright, sunny Southern California summer day. We took off our shirts and swung them over our heads. We cheered like drunken sailors on leave. We listened to our hero Vin Scully echoing from transistor radios throughout the stadium. We'd call out the names of the players and they'd wave back. Wes Parker tipped his hat to us. We chased down foul balls. They truly were six of the finest hours of my entire life. Afterward, we waited and got autographs from Willie Davis, Bill Singer and Al Ferrara!

For thirteen-plus years, life had been methodically teaching me the actual event never meets the anticipated expectation. But this day exceeded all anticipation. The only thing keeping it from being more perfect was the setting sun, sending us onto the freeway onramp and back into our normal lives.

John, I don't know who is happier this day—you or me. I've seen this one coming for a long time. I lined up Koufax to pitch for you. That was no small feat. He was scheduled to face Marichal on Sunday. I had to give Claude Osteen a stiff shoulder so Walt Alston would be forced to move Koufax up a day.

I know you've already discovered much of life isn't as spectacular or satisfying as the anticipation. I've watched this break your heart. It will actually serve to draw you to me. I've built into you this longing for a world which doesn't disappoint. Today, I only wanted to see you enjoying this life as completely as your being can hold. I love you a lot, kid. I can't wait until we get to meet. In the meantime, most of the day-to-day will be fine. You're going to throw a couple no-hitters in high school. Your girlfriend will be prettier than Petula Clark. I've got a trip planned where you and a friend drive up the coast to San Francisco in your dad's Chevy Nova during college spring break. On that trip, I'll have your car break down near Santa Barbara, because I want you to get acquainted with it. You'll live on the beach there in Isla Vista during your wandering years. If you're going to run from me, you might as well live in a nice area.

1966

George Schilling. He was my junior high P.E. teacher—the first adult I can remember hating. Each day he entered the gym with a thick wooden clipboard, wearing a baseball cap with his initials written across it. George A. Schilling. GAS. Appropriate. It's what he gave everyone around him. He was also the first person who taught me the destructive power of appealing to the shame and humiliation of Law.

When I first saw the play *Les Misérables* many years later, I sat spellbound at the unflinching, crushing authority of detective Javert. I was suddenly in the presence of coach Schilling all over again. He thought he could make kids behave by appealing to intimidation. It worked on all of us. None trusted him but all feared him. We also rebelled against him and lied to him, if we thought there was a chance we could get away with it.

He couldn't understand why we played so robotically for him on the flag football team. It was because no one would dare risk creativity, for fear we'd screw up and be publicly humiliated. He didn't realize his methods of turning us against each other in humiliating contests, and public swattings with his wooden clipboard, would actually turn on him.

The power of affirming love is exceedingly greater motivation than what could be gained through intimidation. When we do anything to pacify or appease a disgusted and superior-acting authority, we begin to lose our person. Something sacred inside of us tucks away. We will protect that place more than blocking a blow to our face on the playground.

Schilling taught me to rebel. He taught me that who I was wasn't welcome. He could sense anyone who might be funnier, articulate, or more clever than him. Over time, he would systematically put us down enough to rob it from us.

I won't hate George Schilling as an adult. He was a product of parents and culture teaching a similar, often well-intended devastation. But the spirit behind what drove him crippled millions from my generation. Here is the most damaging reality of that crippling. When we became adults, we found ourselves drawn to teachers and leaders who motivated from similar motivation. They were more handsome, self-assured, and didn't have a scary clipboard. They would have a scary Bible. They would appeal to our flesh, our success, our manhood. They would subtly shame us. Many of us, although we hated it then, will buy their crap now.

1966

If I tell you only what he did wrong, you wouldn't know he was a great dad. For over ten years he quietly woke only me early each Saturday morning. Other fathers would take their sons fishing. My father took me into the kitchen, where the two of us would sit at a linoleum-laminated table, eating a thick concoction of Maypo cereal, whole milk, and serving-spoon scoops of crunchy peanut butter. You could spackle a hole in a wall with the consistency of what we ate.

On summer weekend afternoons, Dad would furtively pull two cans of Vernors out of the refrigerator—like he was handing me a dusty bottle of bootleg rum. It was only ginger ale, but he made it seem so dangerous and forbidden. Each time he'd hand it to me with these words: "Don't tell your mother."

One afternoon, after work, he called me into the living room. He'd put his forefinger through a Dixie cup, and surrounded it with cotton and ketchup. He allowed me to look for a moment directly into the cup, to see a bleeding, wiggling finger.

"A shop worker down at the plant cut off his finger today in one of the sheet metal machines. He told me I could bring it home and let you see it."

He was the most honest man I've known. He sacrificed incredibly for our family. He made sure we visited every state and most of the national parks in the continental U.S. He taught me to compute batting averages with a slide rule.

Before one of our vacation trips, he hid a *MAD* magazine in the glove box. He knew, at some point driving across the country, he would have to discipline me for something ... and he figured we would then both retreat into hurt silence for miles. It, of course, happened. During one hideously long stretch of Midwestern driving monotony, my brother and I began bothering each other in the back seat. He flicked my ear. Twice. So, I tore a page out of what he was reading. He told on me. Dad immediately pulled off the highway. With cars whooshing by us, he completely turned around in his seat and started yelling at me. His face was bright red. He sounded like a TV preacher, bemoaning why they would spend so much money to take vacations so their kids could fight. Next thing I know I was in the front seat across from him. It was all painfully silent and seething ... for what seemed like an hour.

Then, the moment my dad had been waiting for. Driving across the plains of Nebraska, he broke the standoff.

"You might want to check the glove box. Maybe there's something in there that might interest you."

I found the magazine. ... Suddenly, the last fifty miles of angry silence was forgotten. I read him sections all the way into the night, my brother and mom asleep in the backseat, on our way to that evening's Travelodge.

... But my father was a child of the Great Depression, the son of an uneducated immigrant who pushed a fruit cart through their eastern Pennsylvania neighborhood.

Dad was stunningly intelligent. He became a member of Mensa, "The International High IQ Society." He was in the top half of Mensa! He vowed to himself that by dogged diligence and intense focus, he would make himself someone much more financially secure than where he came from. He excelled as navigator on the B-17 bombers, whose accuracy hastened the end of

World War II. He later became deeply respected analytic forecaster at General Electric's headquarters in New York City. He retired as a distinguished economics professor at what is now Thunderbird School of Global Management.

So, here is this nearly genius, high capacity, driven man living his entire life with a fear he'll fall behind and return to the poverty of the Depression.

Awakening: *Parents can unwittingly pass their fear on to their children. It teaches them to perform instead of trust.*

Later I discovered his intelligence reached well beyond his wisdom. He thought intelligence and more education alone would solve the world's problems. I wonder if many extremely intelligent people fail to learn great wisdom because they lack the humility demanded to receive it.

I would rebel against his strict demands and his inability to affirm. His approach would allow him to rarely enjoy who his son actually is—a moderately intelligent dreamer, who loves wistfulness, humor, kindness, affection, affirmation, and talking late into the night. I would become student body president, and an All-State pitcher. I would date the homecoming queen. But it was not the "right" success for him. It would not translate into a law degree from Stanford. I spent too many adolescent years resenting and missing out on enjoying him, because he refused to value or affirm who I actually was. He taught me a lifetime of doubting the value of the particular way I was fashioned.

I may have rejected many of his values, but I inherited most of his prideful fear. Kids from the Depression hated watching their parents be in need of handouts. Dad would not let anyone help him. If someone gave a gift or did a favor, he would quickly try to even the score or surpass it. I'm convinced this transferred fear kept me from letting others in—to see my pain, my weaknesses, my hidden brokenness, and my self-destructive choices.

Later, my dad and I would both grow up. He became an outstanding grandfather. We grew to enjoy each other with deep and tender affection. He would carry his claim of atheism to the grave. He would continue to mock every mention of God, but learn to give my family a pass. He would kindly sit by our nonaluminum tree on Christmas mornings and watch impractical gifts being exchanged, without snide comment. In his last few years on this earth he would say to me: "John, you've done great good in your chosen profession. I've watched how you parent your children and love your wife. You're living this life very well. I'm very proud of you, son. I love you very much."

Not every son gets that blessing. I'm grateful. I wish he could see my children and their own children. He'd be deeply proud of how his name is being lived out in them.

I love my father so much. I'm deeply proud he was my father.

... Jesus whispers,

John, this trust of me you've risked—it has been clumsy and sporadic, but real. I have inhabited it completely. But you will continue to be haunted by patterns you thought you'd someday be freed of. Some of these historic illnesses of your family line may follow you until you leave this earth. But your choice to learn to trust me will protect your family and their families beyond what you can understand now. I know. I've been up ahead. The legacy is being reformed. It fills my heart with joy and my eyes with tears telling you this.

... I too have loved your dad. You can't yet have any idea what transactions people make in their hearts they cannot bring themselves to tell others. Sometimes even Mensa atheists.

1967

My dad gets a big promotion in Phoenix. So, the movers come and pack us up. I still remember; we leave Upland on June 24. And my entire world begins to grow smaller and smaller in the side view mirror of our Chevy Nova. I'm in the back, sitting between our dog and a caged, medicated cat. The after-manufacturer air conditioner stops blowing before we hit Blythe. Our headlights go out shortly after Quartzite. In the car, there's only shocked silence—except for the noise of the highway from our fully opened windows. One of them has my t-shirt taped and flapping in front of it. We soaked it in water back in Blythe. It now forms the centerpiece in our hopes for survival. We must look like a scene from the "Grapes of Wrath." Eventually we stumble into our new city, feeling as though we'd driven a covered wagon through the outskirts of hell. It's ten in the evening and still over one hundred degrees. I already hate every single thing about Phoenix. I can't believe my father would take us from all we've known and bring us here to die. … I clearly express this to him this upon our arrival.

… All this will change in a few weeks, when I meet Jim Adams. He lives three houses down. He owns a bitchen yellow Telecaster guitar and plays songs I've never heard before! He is my introduction into music and all things cool. Half the girls in our neighborhood have a crush on Jim. It's summer and he's bored playing rock and roll all day by himself. He persuades me to take up drums. Promising my parents good grades, I convince them to buy me a set. Although they are purchased at a pawn shop, the snare is a Slingerland and the cymbals are Zildjian. I have, in one purchase, gone from new kid to cool new kid. By the fall, we've formed a band. We name ourselves Metallic Wax. We now must find other musicians worthy of such a moniker. Within several weeks we are joined by Bob Harper on bass and Mark Finezza on rhythm guitar. By the spring of '68 we're one of the better new groups in our surrounding three-block area.

Like kids in open garages all over America, we're learning to make music. I think I'd trade my car and most of my clothing to experience again what that must have been like. I only remember wanting to play all night, working on a song over and over until it worked. It's a moment mediocre garage bands have in common with The Spencer Davis Group, Santana, and Miles Davis.

We play a couple of birthday parties and are promised money for one gig, which later gets cancelled. By March, Metallic Wax has gone the way of Strawberry Alarm Clock. We disband. Sports, girls, and our general lack of talent appear to be our undoing.

But now I have music. I will live with a soundtrack running in the background nearly every waking moment. I will create internal playlists, guiding me through breakups and moments of anticipated greatness. In the fall of 1975, in Tucson, I am limping from a breakup with a girl I thought I'd marry. Neil Young's "Cortez the Killer" mixes with the wind as I wander the desert, searching for the voice of some higher power.

Music becomes the way I will later communicate my life with Jesus. My most intimate, honest and vulnerable moments are spent out in neighborhoods, on beaches, or in cars, alone, making up lyrics and tunes to God. Nothing is more sacred to me.

My formal attempts at sitting and talking to God can feel forced and contrived, often degenerating into what I imagine God might want me to say, in a voice and patter even I don't trust. But when I sing to God, counting on the tune and words to find their way, I am as authentically John as I can be. It usually starts off key and faltering but often moves into a place with God I can find in no other way. I'm trusting God to give me a song so I can stay in the moment long enough to trust him with me.

I wonder in heaven if we get to see scenes we never captured down here. I'd sure like to see the four of us, playing loud and gritty rock and roll, while neighbor kids stop and stare, in awe.

John, I've got several clips of you rehearsing in Finneza's garage. Maybe I should keep looking through the archives. I haven't seen any yet where the neighborhood kids are "staring in awe."

… Sorry. I couldn't help myself.

1967

My brother doesn't join us in Phoenix until later in the summer. He's been working as a counselor at a Boy Scout camp.

Looking back, how do I tell you about my brother Jim?

He's an All-District tennis player, an Eagle Scout, part of the Order of the Arrow. He's my big brother—good, kind and deeply respected. He's my magnificent protector when my humor gets me into trouble with older kids.

Then something happens none of us saw coming. He is sent home from camp early. We thought he'd maybe caught a bad case of flu. But upon his return, we quickly discover something is very, very wrong. Something has snapped inside my brother. He has become mentally ill, deeply psychotic. He suddenly hallucinates, speaks to himself, and has ongoing conversations with others who don't exist. This truly great human will now become part of the best and worst mental health facilities all over the country. My tenderhearted brother will now undergo experimental drugs, shock therapy and the terrifying life away from his home—locked up with others as tormented as him. Like every other family who has ever faced this, we have no idea what to do. That first summer, hoping I can shock him out of his stupor, I actually slug him in the face. It only scares and confuses him more. I still remember him looking shocked, dazed, and hurt. "John, why did you do that?" His rapid decline radically changes our family. We will never be the same.

Since that summer, over forty-five years ago, I've felt like a ticking time bomb, wondering when the same will happen to me. When I get overstressed or Stacey and I get into a hard enough place, I can go there. I fear one day the people who now respect me and enjoy my humor and insight will talk around me, or more slowly, or more loudly. After all, Jim was my brother. Whatever it was came from our line.

Jim passed away seven years ago. This once normal, healthy athlete learned to smoke three packs a day inside mental health facilities where nearly everyone chain smoked. Lung cancer caught up with him. Before it was diagnosed, it had spread all over his body. Within six months my brother was gone.

But one day, in his forties, God worked through the hazy slits in the blinds. My brother allowed in light. I was sitting with him in a restaurant one afternoon, embarrassed by his bursts of loud, inappropriate, crazy talk. On this particular occasion, for a reason I don't yet know, I didn't try to quiet him down. Instead I said, "Jim, there is a place, a land, where no one is mentally ill. My brother, there, in that place, you will be as sharp and awake as any other person." He leaned forward and whispered with lucidity I'd not seen for decades, "Where is this place, John?"

Sitting there over the next hour in that restaurant, I told him nearly everything I knew of Jesus. He asked, "John, how do I get there?" That day he trusted Jesus, and then patiently waited for the day he would take Jim to the land where his mind would work again.

Awakening: *Not all the magnificent heroes get revealed in this lifetime. Some are trapped in bewildering chaos and illness they did not cause. This too is why Jesus came.*

1968

Arlene Ellis is another girl in the crowd. Freshman year she wore braces. But suddenly, today, this first day of school, in Spanish class at Washington High School, I cannot stop looking at her.

"Must-act-now. Must-become-boyfriend-now!"

I've dated several girls before, but this is the first time I will realize I'm not a kid. Several evenings later I risk what seems my entire existence to call her.

This can go so wrong on so many levels. I might become a source of nearly legendary mocking and derision if I screw this up and word gets out. I've never risked anything like this.

Everything has to be exactly right for this call. First, I must find a window of time when my parents aren't home, so I can have run of the family phone and adjoining pacing areas. I've written out a script of what I'll say, with alternate sections depending upon her responses. Now, minutes before the call, a clumsy script rehearsal and a final edit. I have a song selected to play in the background.

If there is a god out there, I promise right now to devote my life to feeding lepers in Nepal, or whatever you'd like, if you'll just cause her to hear me out when I call. I'm willing to follow any god out there who can make this happen. Do you hear me gods? I'm asking only for this one thing!

I'm nearly dry heaving, I'm so nervous. I'm continually shoving back the blinding anxiety, and the utter sense of my universal inadequacy. I dial all but the final number and hang up several times. I fear the first thing she'll hear will be the sound of me clearing my throat. I fear she won't recognize my name.

I dial. I hear the phone ring on her end. She answers. She sounds not unhappy I have called. Somewhere amid my prepared sounding patter, I do manage to slip in that it would be nice to "go get a soda together sometime or something ... um, like to talk over the Spanish assignments." She says she'd "like that."

Did you hear that? She said she'd "like that"!

Now, to get out of the conversation without swearing or sneezing into the phone. I stumble off the call like a blindfolded man maneuvering over a gauntlet of flaming furniture.

I hang up. I am intact! *She and I will be drinking a soda at the same table sometime in the near future. I did it! I am not a loser!* I fist pump my way around the house for the next few minutes, shouting and doing something approximating dance.

In that short, clipped conversation, I become a different person. Over the next several years I will live with a confidence and sense of bearing I have not known before. We will now begin to tell our lives to each other on that phone, for hours, almost every evening. I soon realize I have the capacity to give and receive love. I'm being taught to articulately express affection and affirmation because I need to find exact words to convey the depth of what I am experiencing.

Those first two years are some of the most innocent, playful and winsome days of the first half of my life. I will not know love like this until I am introduced to Stacey Marie Pilger. By then I will be almost mature enough to begin to understand what to do with it.

Jesus says,

So, that promise about devoting your life to whoever could pull it off? Well it wasn't Zeus. I should mention, for the record, you won't make good on your promise. You will ignore many more such promises before we get it right. I've never held you to them.

But you are learning incredible truth these days. You are learning to believe love is indescribably powerful—that it transcends all else. Later, your hungering for a love which refuses to leave when others' loves do will draw you inexorably to me. In the meantime, enjoy. You will spend a lot of money at expensive ice cream shoppes and movie theaters. But you will learn you are lovable—that someone wants to be with you. You will learn you have much love to give and unique ways of expressing it.

When there is no other conflicting issue on the table, I will always defer to giving you the best experiences of joy available. I'm not who you have pegged me. I have loved you completely and perfectly from before the world began.

In the meanwhile, know this: nearly every high school guy resents and admires you for calling her first. Well played, young man, well played.

1969

Pyracantha is nearly irrefutable proof of the existence of Satan. I believe it to be his personal plant of choice. In even the harshest climates it steadily matures into a sticker-hedge of death. I'm almost certain, as a boy, I witnessed a neighbor's dachshund chasing a ball into the pyracantha ... and never coming out. A tiny yelp and then eerie silence. Two hedges of it came with our Phoenix home purchase. Front yard and back. Picture green barbed wire, with inedible red berries.

Trimming it was part of my particular list of "chores." Chores were at the center of the tension between my father and me during high school. He thought I should do them.

I felt strongly I should not.

Especially during summer. I thought I should not be asked to do anything during summer break but stay out long after the streetlights came on.

I was to pick up the dog poop, clean the pool, make my bed, wash the car, mow the lawn, and keep up with the ever-advancing pyracantha. Nearly every day it was the same:

Dad: "John, did you do your chores?"

John: (indistinguishable mumbling)

Dad: "Well, you're not leaving this house until they're done."

John: (louder, nearly distinguishable mumbling)

And so it went. My halfhearted keeping of chores, after enough nagging and threats.

One June morning, this all changed. Before he walked out the door for work, he found me. I was doing nothing, preparing for an entire day of doing nearly nothing.

He was wearing black dress slacks, a starched white shirt and a red tie, held to his shirt with a clip.

"John, I don't tell you enough how much I care about you. You bring a lot of life and laughter to our home. Your mom and I are so proud of you. Do you know that?" Then he headed to the door, turning back to say, "If you want, when I get home, we could play some catch."

Then he was off. So were my plans for the rest of the day. I still don't know what happened. Did he take a parenting class the evening before? Regardless, almost involuntarily, I walked to our shed and pulled out our hedge trimmers. They were rusted and jammed. I had no gloves. I poured a jug of water and walked out into the Phoenix summer heat to tackle the hellish pyracantha.

I dug deep into that spreading vine of death. I reshaped that ignored mass of thorns into something almost resembling a manicured hedge. It took me almost all day. I didn't care. I don't think I'd ever worked so hard. My hands were blistered from the antique hedge trimmer and my arms were bleeding from picking up thorn-covered vines formed during the Hoover administration. I took garbage can after garbage can to the alley and mowed up the last scraps I couldn't get by hand.

I was in my bedroom when I heard his '62 Chevy station wagon turn into the carport. Mom greeted him at the door. "Jim, you have to come and see what John did today!" Through the mostly closed blinds on my bedroom window, I watched him walk out to inspect what I'd done.

Then, the reason I had cancelled a summer day with buddies. He smiled. I rarely got to see that smile. He was beaming. He was proud of his son. I was getting to be the son he described to me before he left for work.

A rebellious high school kid turned friend in one interchange. Though my dad didn't have God as his motivation, something about being formed in the very image of God caused him to affirm

and bless a son who less than deserved it. And that son found himself wanting to bring great joy to his father.

Awakening: *The motivation of grace will always bear greater fruit than the coercion of demand.*

1971

The moment I first see Koufax I want to be a great pitcher. I never worked at anything as hard. I give up all other sports by my junior year and concentrate on whatever I can do to become an All-State pitcher and help Washington High win a state title. In the offseason I run up mountains and lift weights. Most free moments I roll a ten-pound weight, attached with rope to a stick, up and down, to strengthen the muscles in my pitching hand. My parents allow me to build a mound in our back yard. I cement two beams sixty feet and six inches away and hang a mattress between them. I pitch thousands of baseballs into the square I draw onto it. I can still hear the thud of a fastball hitting that thrift-store mattress.

Spring of 1971 surpasses even my dreams.

In my first six games I throw two no-hitters, a one-hitter, a two-hitter and two three-hitters. I'm striking out two batters an inning! As a lefthander, I'm averaging a pickoff a game. I dream about setting up a hitter with a high, inside fastball and punching him out with a low and away curve that will buckle his knees. I'm copying what I've watched Koufax do all those years—with his same high leg kick.

One June morning, I'm reading the sports page and I turn to the feature article titled, "The Arizona All-State Baseball Team." I search for my name. ... There it is.

"John Lynch, left-handed pitcher. Washington High School."

My mom walks through the neighborhood with scissors to capture as many copies of the article as possible. Life feels about perfect this day. ...

But, when you're dreaming a dream, you often don't see past the moment of its realization. You see it happening and imagine all manner of stupendous good following it. But it doesn't always work like that. Even dreams coming true often carry an ugly asterisk next to them.

The Arizona All-State game in 1971 is played at the Cleveland Indians' spring-training stadium. In the rows behind home plate are dozens of scouts with speed guns monitoring everything in front of them. I pitch second for the North team and don't allow a hit over my two innings. I'm hoping I've done enough for someone to draft me.

After the game, a scout for the Giants finds me. "John, that was a mighty fine performance out there tonight. I've got to talk to some folks upstairs, but I think we're going to take you in the draft next month."

I stood there frozen ... with my dad, some friends, and a scout for the San Francisco Giants! It seemed too good to be true.

It was ...

He ended with the words, "All right, John Pierson, keep your nose clean. You'll hear from us."

John Pierson?

The scout had mistaken me for John Pierson, my teammate from Washington High, who had also played in this game. The John Pierson who was once a close friend. The John Pierson who had recently stolen away my girlfriend.

That John Pierson.

By reflex I got out the words, "Um, I'm not John Pierson. I'm John Lynch."

"Oh, sorry. Could you point out John Pierson to me?"

I did.

As my friends found excuses to leave that moment, my dad and I began to make our way out from under the lights and into the dark neighborhoods where our car was parked. Nothing was spoken. But another layer of shame got added to the story, which begins with the words, "Lynch, there is something uniquely and particularly wrong with you."

For the rest of my life, I have watched many versions of that story get played out. It kicks the wind out of you. If you know God, it can twist your picture of him.

As long as I believed God's goal for my life should be painless and smooth, with only happy endings, I would live in a cognitive dissonance, which would make me pull back and protect myself. I can slip into dangerous thinking that if he's good and powerful, our lives should be smoother and less messy than others. Bad guys should lose more often. Good guys, with a big curve and a dream should most often win. Sometimes it works that way. Often it does not. Not yet.

God apparently allows some of the pain of a fallen world to get through to us—believer or not. It's what he does with the pain and bad endings that ultimately proves his love and goodness. If he is able to take all of the twisted mess that finds us and is somehow able to turn it all into our good, that would be something very amazing indeed. For all the accusation he has promised too much, this is exactly what he says he is doing. "I will cause all things to work together for good" … for the likes of us.

That night at the All-State game made no sense to me. *How can something I worked this hard for end up more painful than having never tried anything at all?*

His answer to this question will come decades after this game, only after I've trusted him with the answer.

John, I watch how hard you try to continue to draw near to me, even as I allow things into your life which utterly exasperate you. You're clinging to the belief that I am fully for you, and care more about you than you do. Then something happens which seems to undermine it all … I know. I watch. It deeply hurts me to watch you experience such disappointment and a broken heart. You might try to let me off the hook by reasoning I'm not fully in control of your world. Such thinking might maintain a measure of your affection for me—like giving a pass for a grandfather who loves you but can't always remember your name. But this lie will ultimately ruin our relationship. I am fully in control of your world. There is nothing that happens, doesn't happen, refused, or delayed without me seeing it, or allowing it. I am in control of your life. And I love you more than you love you. My character cannot and will not do wrong. I take whatever your race has brought on, and I redeem, refashion, and rework it all into beauty beyond anything you could have possibly imagined. All things. Horrible things. Evil things. Chronic things. I decide what is allowed through and what it will accomplish. I decide what needs to be refashioned. But mostly I stand in the arena, when you cannot stand, defending you and protecting you. I do not lecture; I do not mock. What I do is love you, no matter how angry you are at me, no matter what you imagine in your heart about me. I enter into your pain more deeply than even you. This I can do. This I will always do. Until we are home together in the land where tears cease.

1972

It was always about playing hard, and coming home tired with enough memories of glory to sustain our dreams. It was always about laughing hard and having a great adventure. When we were done with the day, we'd lie on our backs in cool grass, with our arms folded behind our heads, staring at clouds, and retelling to each other a version of a game much better than what actually happened. In my neighborhood, nobody talked about discipline or taking it seriously. But we played harder, enjoyed it more, and had each other's back better than any organized team we will ever play on after it.

That's why it hurt so badly to get trashed by a coach for enjoying it so much when I got to college.

I had scholarships to other schools after high school, but Arlene Ellis chose Arizona State University. So, without a scholarship and way over my head, I continued my boyhood dreams at ASU, under coach Bobby Winkles. He was the man! A legendary backwoods, tobacco-spitting, old-school coach, he had turned Arizona State from nearly intramural baseball to a program yearly competing for an NCAA national championship.

He liked me. He appreciated my passion and love of the game. He started me in center field one practice game. He rarely put pitchers in other positions. I hit the first pitch from Dale Hrovatt over the center field fence at Goodwin Stadium! Next inning, I misplayed a fly ball, and was back to pitching. But still! I don't think I ever enjoyed playing for a coach as much.

But in those days, the freshmen were coached primarily by the assistant coach. … He enjoyed me not much at all.

I was surrounded by nationally recruited, blue-chip, flame-throwing sensations; most would go onto long major-league careers. I was now a junk-throwing local kid with a damaged shoulder and a memory of a fastball. I shouldn't have tried to hang on. But I wasn't ready to leave the game. I'd thrown some surprisingly good winter ball stints in relief. I still thought I'd make it back and would get drafted in late rounds.

But mostly, baseball was still fun to me. Warming up is nearly every ballplayer's favorite part of the sport. The fifteen minutes before drills, batting practice, fielding, and inter-squad games. It was our refuge—from schoolwork, from responsibility, from the looming seriousness of life.

Each of us had warmed up thousands of times in ball fields all over the country. We knew that ball-hitting-glove sound like our own voices. It was therapy and a theme park all at once. This is where the best humor came out. We'd mock each other. We'd work on our invented knuckleballs. (All college ball players think they can throw a knuckleball). We'd turn our gloves inside out. We chewed tobacco and sang jingles from commercials. We'd talk trash about each other's girlfriends. … And, in a raw and clumsy way, we learned to have each other's back. We knew when to get serious. All of us did. But as time honored as any unwritten baseball rule, screwing around while getting loose has always been near the top.

At least I thought so.

In one of our routine team meetings, sitting on the grass in the outfield, the assistant coach wanted to talk about "discipline and taking things seriously." He chose me as the scapegoat to make his point. He tore me apart in front of my friends and fellow ballplayers.

"Lynch, you think you're so damned funny. You think everything's a joke. You know how to get others to screw around, until my good players forget why we brought them here. Lynch, you're like a cancer to a team. Did you all hear me? Players like Lynch are a cancer. They poison the water and others don't even notice it. Well, that's not the way we won a national championship when I played first base here, and it's not the way we're going to play ball now, dammit! So, Lynch, you decide what you are—a ballplayer or a comedian. … All right, everyone, get to work."

It's a uniquely horrible feeling to be shamed as an athlete. Something in your masculinity, in your very person gets diminished. The respect and hard-earned trust between ballplayers is experienced at every level. We were used to getting called out for not running hard on an infield popup. But none of us were prepared to have our personhood attacked. This coach knew what he was doing. He was ostracizing me from the rest of the team. Hanging out with me would risk becoming this coach's next target.

That was the last day I would enjoy playing baseball. I would leave the game forever three weeks later.

John, I formed you to encourage community—to affirm, bless, enjoy, and bring out the best in others. When you run up against an insecure person who can coach only by threatening and belittling, your motive will always be misunderstood. And you will get hurt.

This moment will help develop a conviction you will teach for the rest of your life; people work best and hardest in a place where they know they are valued.

I am going to surround you with some strong friend, who will protect you as you model and teach this way of life.

None of this will help you much for about twenty years. What happened today will wound you. You will have no one to protect you. Until this moment, you have respected and obeyed even bad authority. But this will change you. It will give you increasing permission to mistrust all authority. You are about to enter a brutally hard time of your life.

I'm here. One day, you'll understand I suffered under insecure authority which ultimately tried to destroy one who would threaten it with good. You're in good company today. You just don't know it yet.

By the way, that coach, he knows he's wrong. He will go home after today's practice and sit in front of a television set and know he's wrong. You'll be teaching this way of life to his sons and daughters. Hold on, kid.

Awakening: *In an environment of law, every motive is suspect. In an environment of grace, good motive is presumed.*

October 1972

We are out to dinner this evening, Arlene and I. Recently, things have not been going well with us. But nothing has prepared me for the words she says to me tonight. ...

"John, I think we should break up."

She has seen enough. She has known me for six years now. We've been together almost every day. She loves me and deeply enjoys me. But I am too much work. I have not learned how to be secure dating this uncommonly beautiful girl. She has grown weary of defending herself. My insecurity and shame are now disrupting my world at its very core.

How hard it must have been for her to prepare to say those words! How long did she know and not tell me, afraid of hurting me? In the moment, I'm not mature enough to tell her how brave she is.

Everything happening next is a frantic blur. I pay the check before our meal arrives and drive her home in the rain. Neither of us speaks a word. There is only the sound of windshield wipers, mocking me. I drop her off and stare at her one more time before she walks out of my sight.

I drive wildly back to the fraternity. My best friend is not in his room. I bang on his door like a deranged man, yelling at the top of my lungs. Then, in my shiny white shoes and dress slacks, I run through the streets of Tempe, moaning out loud, "This time it is really over."

As long as she was in my world, I could make sense of life. She was not only a girlfriend. Her affirmation and smile were how I knew who I was. Now suddenly I am alone. Another thick layer of shame is being formed on that run. To have someone know me up close for a long, long time. For that person to know the deepest, most real truths about me, to know my dreams, my secrets, my weaknesses ... and then choose to no longer be with me. To not be enough for that person. *Where do I go? What do I do with the rest of this life? Who is built to withstand such pain?*

I discover myself in a park, miles away, panting and drenched.

Awakening: *Rejection can tempt me to spend the rest of my life proving I'm worth loving. But it will never convince me.*

The most darkness-defying risk a human can take is to believe, even in this moment, this is true: In my freshly proven shame and sense of failure, I want to turn away from it. But to do so is to deny the reason Jesus went to the cross.

On my worst day I am: adored, enjoyed, clean, righteous, absolutely forgiven, new, acceptable, complete, chosen, able, intimately loved, smiled upon,
planned for, protected, continually thought about, enjoyed, cared for, com-
forted, understood, known completely, given all mercy, compassion, guarded,
matured, bragged on, defended, valued, esteemed, held, hugged and caressed,
kissed, heard, honored, in unity with, favored, enough, on time, lacking nothing, directed, guided continually, never failed, waited for, anticipated, part of,
belonging, never alone, praised, secure, safe, believed, appreciated, given all
grace, all patience, at peace with, pure, shining, precious, cried over, grieved
with, strengthened, emboldened, drawn kindly to repentance, relaxed with,
never on trial, never frowned at, never hit with a two-by-four, at rest in, receiving complete access, given gifts, given dreams, given new dreams, continually
healed, nurtured, carried, never mocked, never punished, most of my humor
enjoyed, not behind, not outside, given endless affection.

It doesn't always much feel like it in the moment. This is the depth of His love,
whether you or I feel we deserve it or not. "Deserve" has long ago left the building.

1973

The combination of Arlene leaving and my baseball career ending do me in. Within a few months my clothing styles change. I grow my hair long and I move out of the fraternity. Without debate, I give myself permission to live a life I previously never considered. I spend more time with an older friend, who introduces me into a counterculture lifestyle. I'm eating tofu and lentil beans with curry. Soon I'm trying out TM and studying the teachings of Baba Ram Dass. I'm checking out nearly every hip manner of spirituality I can locate. I'm now smoking pot daily and will soon aggressively plow my way through all manner of psychedelic drugs. I'm reading Carlos Castaneda, Richard Brautigan, Kurt Vonnegut, and *Zen and the Art of Motorcycle Maintenance.* I try dating girls I knew from the sororities, but my heart's not in it. They're far too much part of the "establishment" for my new thinking.

Dad has taken a promotion to General Electric headquarters in Connecticut. The next time my parents see me, I will present an entirely different son. One of my strong regrets is forcing them to react to my new directions instead of giving them the gift of walking with me through it. I will do this to them over and over through the next decades. Near the end of his life, my dad will tell me he wished I hadn't imposed my newfound faith as a line-in-the-sand declaration. "Do you know how hard it is for your son to defiantly tell you he now believes differently than you, without ever giving you the chance to enter the conversation?"

John, you are trying to navigate life without anyone standing next to you. You are afraid of being hurt. You think you are more open-minded, but are actually closed to everything but bluffing. You are open to all manner of lies. You will try nearly everything, except me. Tonight, as you lie in bed, I am trying to help you know I'm here. I'm not angry, I'm not disgusted. I'm waiting. This next part of this story will be horribly hard. But I promise, I will not let a minute of it be wasted. After it is all over, you will wake up and still be right on time.

1973

In two semesters, I change my major from Political Science, to Psychology, to Recreation, then English. My major at this moment is Speech Communication, with a minor in Drama. In the theater, I discover the vehicle I will communicate from for much of the rest of my life. In my first acting class I discover an uncommon ability to bring printed words alive on a stage. I discover a professor and mentor named Dr. Witt. He's a short, rumpled, pudgy man in his fifties, with a bushy mustache and wild hair. He's an eccentric, brilliant, accomplished stage actor and director. I have been spellbound, watching him act and direct actors.

In his Beginning Acting class I perform a soliloquy from *Long Day's Journey into Night*. As soon as I sit down, he dramatically pops up, and slithers up close to the class. He puts his forefinger to his lips, tilts his head to the side, and whispers:

"Shh … For a moment, try to absorb what happened. That, right there. What you just watched. That was acting! This is why I love teaching. For moments like this. Where someone with no training shows up and brings something alive and real to this stage. The rest of you dullards move from one piece of furniture to another, reciting words as from a recipe card. This young man made me believe him. He believed himself. Whatever it is he understands, the rest of you need to discover. Or your only role in the theater will be as prop-handlers in a cafetorium production of *Pippen*."

… I sit there staring, realizing in that moment, this is the gift I would carry for the rest of my life. I only needed another to see it in me.

I love everything about taking on a character: the preparation, the memorization, blocking, self-directing, getting into character, and then playing it all out in front of others. No net. The audience and actors create a moment which wouldn't exist otherwise. Both are indispensible to the other. The only movie where I've seen this truth captured is *Shakespeare in Love*. We are watching the beginning of the first ever performance of *Romeo and Juliet*. It is sputtering out of the gate. The play is given up on by nearly everyone within five minutes.

… Then a vulnerable line is believably delivered. And a spark catches. In moments, the audience is now trying, through nodding and leaning, to call out to the actors: "We're here. We've bought in. We've got you. Run with this! We'll catch you if you fall. Please, give us something which will help us transcend our lives. We will do our part." The actors soon find their footing. A permission from trust has been forged. Something palpable and tangible, wild and unbridled is being created that never existed before this moment. Everyone knows magic is happening, and no one will allow this spell to be broken. …

I'm not really an actor, at least not in the classical sense. I just think I am comfortable being John Lynch in different outfits. I can convince you I believe I am who I am portraying. That's all it takes for an audience to buy in and allow you to take them to another place, to another way of seeing.

Theater is not only what takes place on a stage. You don't have to be an actor to pull out a memory and bring it to those who were not there. Whenever that takes place, something magical happens. It's the key to great teaching, storytelling, parenting, songwriting, or opening your heart. To take yourself back into a redemptive moment and replay it. It inspires and frees others. It's about as close as transcending into the eternal as we get down here. When you can get out of the way of your self-consciousness long enough to convince another you are there in the moment, it allows them to be transported to places they might otherwise never get to go. ... All of it is exceedingly life-giving.

With all the pain and ugliness of what is coming up, I remain grateful that God uses this time to teach me how to be me in front of others. I learn a craft I will get the privilege to perform the rest of my life, to one day help free others into grace.

You will never be able to quickly tell a wrench from a pair of pliers. You will never successfully work on anything electrical your entire life. But this I have given you to do. Do you know how much I enjoy watching you unwind a piece, while I sit in the audience with others, allowing myself to be transported into the scene you create? Yes, me. That's what love does. It trusts another to benefit from who they are. Bravo, my friend. Bravo!

1975

No money I've ever possessed was spent as well as the $225 I paid for that blue 1960 ragtop VW Bug.

I graduated from college in May. While most of my friends were transitioning into careers they'd been interning for, I pointed that car and her misfiring cylinders toward Santa Barbara. Several years before, during a spring break trip, the fuel pump in my '65 Chevy Nova went out and had to be repaired in Isla Vista, outside of Santa Barbara. I spent three days there with a friend. I drove away in love with all things beach town.

For the next several years I lived with only what my VW could carry as I waited tables from Santa Barbara to Laguna Beach.

I developed a predictable pattern: show up into a new town, sleep in my car, find a waiter's job, move in with other waiters. I loved being the winsome new guy with stories to tell of the open road. I was made for waiting tables! You're given money for helping others enjoy their time. For a performer, that's easy money. We ate the food guests left on their plates. At a nice steak and fish house you could score lobster, crab and steak all evening long. Ramen during the day; surf and turf at dinner.

I stayed in each town until things got too complicated. Then I'd pack up Blue and move on.

I loved my car. I drove her long distances, mostly at night. She couldn't handle the desert during the day. I propped up the engine cover an inch or so with a fishing rod, so she wouldn't vapor lock. My 6-volt battery spent more time dead than alive. I learned to park on slants, so later I could push her with the driver's door open, hop in, drop into second gear, lurch her into life, and off down the road. A hippie's dream.

I'd drive through the night, with her ragtop wide open, creating radio talk shows. I made up an imaginary talk show host, who'd take calls from all manner of imaginary people.

"Hello, this is Bob Abernathy. You're on the air. What's your gripe; what's your complaint?"

"Yep, Bob, thanks for the handle. I'm Floyd McCutcheon. I'm driving a big rig outta Sioux

Falls, heading to Barstow on a blind flip to Chi town."

"What you carrying, Floyd?"

"Bearings, Bob. Lateral cinch bearings for farm equipment. You use 'em to modulate your flash point while galvanizing sheet metal into bevel housing conduits. Try torquing an aftermarket adaptor without cinch bearings and you'll be pulling rivets out of your Ditch Witch like silt from a frontload grain harvester. You know what I mean, Bob?"

"So, Floyd, what's your gripe; what's your complaint?"

"Well, Bob, it's this whole liberal, Trilateral Commission nonsense. I don't see how we can sit by and watch these Commies slip through the slats, like so many cam-adaptor freeze plugs. Next thing you know, Congress'll be letting them special interest groups sell our children to outsourced plantation bosses in Paraguay. You know what I mean, Bob?"

… There is no accent or voice I use today who didn't first call in to Bob Abernathy's show.

That car taught me to love road trips, seek out diners, enjoy cow-shaped creamers, eat pie, make small talk with locals, smell night air, watch stars over me, form new dialects, and be comfortable alone, with myself … driving along, waiting to meet Everyman.

I still love all of it.

Awakening: *God enjoys the tastes and enjoyments I cultivated in my unbelieving days. He only wants to enjoy them with me and discard the ones that hurt me.*

John, when you were forced to sell Blue for rent money back in Connecticut, I made sure she had a great final owner. An older widow in upstate New York. She saw the car sitting in front of a Chinese restaurant with a For Sale sign on the front windshield. She'd driven past it every day for months. She loved that car. She used to be a hairstylist for the Yardbirds. The bass player had one the same color you repainted yours. One day she said to me, "If that car is still there a month from now, I'm going to take it as a sign you'd like me to have it." People are throwing that kind of nonsense at me all the time. I don't want to encourage it. Next thing I know, I'm being asked to make the sunset a certain color. Anyway, for her, I made an exception. I wanted your car to have a great last home. I'm sentimental like that. So sue me.

For ten years she drove that beauty from her farm outside Mount Kisco into town and back. Her dogs loved the open top. They put their paws on the back of the front seats and stuck their heads out the top of the car. The car never had a repair. I thought you should know.

1977

Early on I drove with friends to Las Vegas. Later I got a ride with near strangers. Eventually, I hitchhiked by myself.

I still don't know why Vegas draws me. I've been told a dozen reasons why it shouldn't. Maybe it's because I started going there back in the early '70s, when attractive cocktail waitresses would come to your chair at the slot machines and kindly offer you immense free shrimp cocktails.

Even the bathrooms were over the top. Every casino on the Strip had bathroom valets! They would buff shoes, light cigarettes, or whisk suit coats. I always wished I could borrow a coat, so I could get a whisking and maybe a story from one of those friendly old black gents. Each had an entire table of elegant and expensive male grooming accoutrements: witch hazel, hair sprays and gels, mouthwash, deodorant, cologne, gum. And combs waiting in a giant cylinder of bright-blue sanitizer. It was all so completely opposite of my wooden-crate décor of madras curtains and beanbag chairs. It was so completely otherworldly for me—a flannel-shirt-wearing hippie in this sparkly leisure-suit town.

I had the bad fortune of winning five hundred dollars the first time I went. I thought this was how Vegas worked. But, almost every following trip, through college and beyond, I would wager and eventually lose most of my money for the month. I learned in those days how to live on potato salad for weeks at a time.

My first time there was for a tournament with the Phoenix American Legion Baseball All-Stars. I was eighteen, and still wearing braces, but somehow I found myself seated at a blackjack table inside the Sahara. In those days, at a corner of each table, they provided a clear plastic bin of non-filtered cigarettes. I loved all the freebies. So I tried one. I figured it might help me look older. I ordered a Harvey Wallbanger, because it's what the guy next to me was drinking. Then I put a Lucky Strike into my mouth. I didn't light it. I only wanted to look like I belonged at a place where filterless cigarettes are an anticipated choice.

Cigarettes and braces are a bad combination. The dealer could see it all happening right in front of him. I was oblivious. It was the middle of the afternoon. There was an attractive young woman, several seats away at this two-dollar table. I glanced over at her, like I'm the drummer for a band playing somewhere tonight on the Strip. If she had looked over, she would have seen my braces covered and my chin wet with Lucky Strike tobacco—dripping onto my shirt.

Whenever I think I'm somebody more than I am, the dealer's words from that afternoon come back to me:

"Son, I'm going to have to ask you to put what's left of that cigarette into the ashtray. You're getting wet tobacco all over my table. And you might want to check your smile in the restroom mirror."

… But on this particular day, seven years later, I'm outside Wickenburg, trying to look nonthreatening, hoping to catch a ride to Caesar's Palace. After about an hour, a giant Cadillac slows past me and honks for me to get in. There are giant cattle horns on the front hood of this jet-black beauty. As I slide in, the driver smiles, tips his giant cowboy hat and growls in a deep, raspy Texan voice, "Howdy, young man. The name's Laramie Jordan."

Laramie Jordan. It's a stage name that stuck for him. He tells me he used to have a local television show, "The Laramie Jordan Show," back in the late '50s on KPHO. From the moment I get in until he drops me off before disappearing into the Caesar's Palace private underground parking garage, he never stops talking. A friendly, washed-up semi-celebrity, wanting someone to hear stories from when he ruled the airwaves.

He buys me lunch in Kingman. "Order whatever you like, young fella."

He never asks anything about me. But before he drops me off he says this:

"Young fella, you have a great time. Live it up. Don't even think about the consequences. But on the day you turn thirty, I want you to look into the mirror and take stock of who are you. You hear me young man? Thirtieth birthday. You remember old Laramie Jordan told you to do it. All right. Time for you to get out of the car. Mama needs a new pair of snakeskin boots!"

He tips his hat and is gone. I never see him again.

That night I play blackjack and drink whisky for hours and hours. I turn two hundred dollars into sixteen hundred dollars, and then back to zero dollars. I vividly remember walking out of the casino, angry with myself for not being able to stop.

What's wrong with you? Who are you? What are you going to do now? It's the thirteenth and you don't get any more money until the start of the month. How are you going to explain this back home? Why do you do this? Are you sick?

I lie down in the grass out near the pool at the Sands casino and pass out. I awake several hours later, sopping wet from sprinklers, which moments ago turned on. I stumble to my feet and find my way to a road leading me out of town.

It's one thing to be a college kid going up for a weekend to Las Vegas with buddies. It's very much another to be completely alone, having lost all my money for the month, sopping wet, swearing at myself, trying to thumb a ride in the middle of the night. I have no more illusions of my imperviousness to misfortune.

... I am now not that far from God.

On the day I turn thirty, I will be a believer, in seminary—sane, sober, and taking second-year Greek. And because Laramie Jordan told me to five years earlier, I will find myself that evening, looking into the bathroom mirror, and almost involuntarily taking stock of who I am. ...

Thank you, Laramie Jordan.

1978

… And God makes his first entrance.

I was waiting for him to show up again all my life. I just wasn't sure who it was. Jackson Browne sang, "… waiting here for Everyman." I was now desperately waiting, holding on. I didn't know it was him I was waiting for.

Jesus.

Oh, how the very name freaked me out. Growing up with my atheist, socialist dad, Jesus was blamed for every societal weakness … and for creating Republicans. All Christians were uneducated, snake-handling frauds, whose ancestors started every war.

Still, I am searching the landscape. The American Dream has now completely slipped the rails. The homecoming queen is gone. My All-State pitching hand is stained yellow from cigarettes. I live in growing paranoia, imagining every cop knows about the bag of weed stuffed under my passenger seat.

I'm now in Laguna Beach, living with a girl in an apartment on the Coast Highway. On this particular spring Saturday we decide to see a movie. The main beach theater is playing *Oh, God!* It's a simplistic comedy about God, living incognito, on earth. God is played by George Burns, a deadpan, crotchety old vaudeville actor. He portrays God as a cigar smoker with a dry wit and a willingness to admit he made the avocado pit too large. Something about the picture of a God willing to poke fun at himself flips a switch inside me.

I can't speak as I walk out of the theater. She asks what's wrong. I can't tell her. I don't know. We walk across the street and through the lobby of a hotel and out to the balcony overlooking the Pacific Ocean. We order wine. It's silent for a while.

And there, right then, hope tops the horizon. For the second time in my life I am overwhelmed with the all-encompassing presence of the God of the universe. It's consistently as strong, certain and pure as those two minutes at age eleven.

… Hold on kid. It won't be long now.

In that moment, staring out into the setting sun, I begin sobbing.

In that same moment, the woman I'm sitting across from is probably pondering which new guy she'll now be moving in with. …

1979

I'm back in Phoenix, teaching high school Drama and English. It's been a year since the God experience on the balcony in Laguna. Over these months, I've gradually tried to rationalize it all as the mystical experience of emotions mixed with a movie, wine, and a sunset. The Laguna Beach girl decides to move to Phoenix with me, convinced I'm over my Jesus moment. But lately, I'm listening to an album a friend has given me. Keith Green is a Christian songwriter who once played piano in a band on the Sunset Strip. It's the first Christian album I've heard which doesn't sound like Muzak or funeral home music.

I've started to read the Bible. I'm mostly reading the words in red. Jesus is coming off as the coolest hippie ever! He's telling the crowds not to worry about how they're gonna make ends meet. Like it's all gonna work out. He says the birds don't worry about things and yet God knows when any of them fall from the sky. I discover he knows how many hairs are on everyone's head. I'm not sure why he wants to know this, but I'm impressed. I watch him care for the sick and walk into bars to hang out with the dregs of society.

I'm at the exact place millions get to. I'm becoming drawn to Jesus, but the hurdles to him seem insurmountable. I have too many questions, like …

1. How could this man Jesus be God? That's like saying spinach dip is a barn owl.
2. There's not enough whisky to believe God would come to earth as a baby, through a woman.
3. The resurrection is creepy, sci-fi sounding stuff. Nowhere in my world does anything like that happen.
4. How can a book this old, written by fallible humans, ever be trusted?
5. His followers, almost to a person, come off as pretentious, bluffing, superstitious kooks, who dress like they have a date with a covered wagon.
6. I'd have to give up dope. I am not giving up dope.
7. Their music makes one wish the synthesizer had never been invented.
8. I don't have the energy to bluff better behavior.
9. Christian television.
10. I will not play the fool and believe a religious opiate. I must hold out on my search for truth.

Not trying to rub it in. But you will, one day, have to give answers to this stuff for others like you. Again, only an observation…

1979

God moments are starting to happen more and more often now.

A friend asks me to join him to get out of town for a couple of days. He knows some lawyer friends in San Diego who will put us up. We drive in Friday evening, joining them for dinner, drinks and several joints. These guys are well-read, brilliant, immensely funny. Eventually the conversation gets around to mocking Jesus and Christians. This has been a common default subject in my world for a long time. But for the first time, I can't join in. Suddenly, these lawyers seem like the simpletons, with their tired approach of marginalizing God by mocking the most bizarre of his followers. All three notice I'm not taking part. My friend asks me what's going on. I think to myself, *I can no longer mock him.*

I find myself saying, "You ever read about him? I've been reading a Bible recently. I don't want to make fun of him anymore. If any of what they've written is true, he was a pretty remarkable person. If you could hear yourselves, it all sounds so petty and small. Like we're mocking because we're afraid it could be true. It's like we're all afraid of something, or we'd leave it alone."

My friend is now glaring at me, knowing I've ruined our chance at two nights in San Diego. We probably got in the car and headed back to Phoenix. I did know I had crossed a line. I was now in between worlds—no longer belonging anywhere.

John, I don't know if you can understand how profoundly beautiful it is to me, what you did. You were defending me. You were hurt for me. You risked alienation to have my back. Thank you. I will not forget this evening.

1979

I am sitting on my bed, listening to a Bob Dylan album. Dylan is my generation's prophet. He has been on more covers of *Rolling Stone* than any individual musician. Twenty-five minutes ago I pulled *Slow Train Coming* from its album jacket and put the turntable needle to vinyl. I had no idea what to expect. There are rumors Dylan has embraced a new faith. I listen without moving, for the entire album side, crying and sighing like I might stop breathing. The needle skips at the end for several minutes before I again realize where I am. The last song, "When He Returns," has left me ruined.

Surrender your crown on this bloodstained ground, take off your mask
He sees your deeds, He knows your needs even before you ask
How long can you falsify and deny what is real?
How long can you hate yourself for the weakness you conceal?
Of every earthly plan that be known to man, He is unconcerned
He's got plans of his own to set up His throne
When He returns.

Then,

... For all those who have eyes and all those who have ears It is
only He who can reduce me to tears.

Before the day is over I will have played both sides half a dozen times. God uses Dylan to crumble my last wall. To hear him sing these words tells me the old order is being swallowed up. The renegades and chain-smokers are being invited in. If Dylan could pen this love, maybe it's for me too. ...

The rest of the way is paperwork. My weakness is about to become unconcealed. ...

John, back in 1966 I had Claude Osteen's shoulder stiffen up so you could see Koufax. Today I have timed Bob Dylan's journey to meet yours in this cold room on Thirty-sixth Street, north of Thomas. I put this all together before the world began. I love you this much. I know how your heart works; I knew exactly the timing for this regeneration. I promised you it would not be much longer. You will read The Great Divorce by Lewis and watch Jesus of Nazareth early this Christmas season. Several more of your students will talk with you about me. A total stranger will stop you in a mall and tell you about me. You will be surprised you let him. You will meet him again one day. He's an angel.

… I would leave December 23 open.

December 20, 1979

I still smoke.

In college I played a character who smoked. By the time the play ended I was in for two packs a day. Nothing has ever confused me as much as my relationship with smoking. I love everything about smoking. And nothing I do disgusts me more. It's been five years now of trying to stop. I've done almost everything. Several times I actually did it—stopped, cold turkey. For months. Then something would hit and I'd give myself permission to light up again. It's maddening. I do not understand me. Why would I do something I hate, once finally freed from it? I can't understand how I could stop for several months, and then start again because a friend on a boat offers me a cigarette.

One evening last month I'm sitting in my living room late at night—miserable and angry I still haven't quit. I stare at the last cigarette from my carton's last pack of Marlboros. I yell out this promise to myself:

"This, right here, right now, is the last cigarette I will ever smoke! I'm not playing a game this time. This is for real. This is my last smoke! … Goodbye my old friend."

I flip her into the air and catch her deftly between my first and second finger—an impressive skill I've learned over the last sixty thousand cigarettes. I caress her gently like you would a lover you're about to leave. I'm trying to savor every moment of this—from the strike of the match to the crackling sound of tobacco meeting flame. I deftly form thick, nearly perfect smoke rings and then watch them float across the room, gently losing their integrity. I replay all the moments I've done this dance—in my Volkswagen, in motel rooms, after great meals, in a sleeping bag next to a girlfriend, waking up on the beach. I slowly savor her down to the nub. Then, benevolently, I lay her down and let her burn out on her own. A kind gesture of appreciation. And then … I am done. A new day is dawning.

For good measure I scrunch up all the cigarette stubs in the ashtray, and pour beer over them. It smells lousy, but it convinces me this time I actually mean it.

I crawl into bed … a free man.

Next morning I awaken … a crazed man.

I am freaking desperate for a smoke! I completely brush aside my promise from last evening, like lint off a coat.

The internal conversation goes like this:

I know I made a promise, but I didn't know I was going to feel like this! I can't live like this. Nobody can live like this! People on death row at least have smokes! I need to get into a better state of mind! I'll try it again, once I'm back in a stable relationship. I mean it. But right now I gotta have a smoke!

I can't find any. I remember last night's final cigarette was from my last pack. I'm panicked, now scrambling around looking under furniture, inside coat pockets. It's a two-minute drive to a convenience store, but I won't make it. I need a smoke now!

Then, I look over at the ashtray. Without even a thought, I rush over and start straightening out the crumpled cigarette butts of last night. *I think they're actually dried enough to light!* Hunched over the ashtray in my underwear, I light up the stubs of beer-flavored cigarettes. … I take a deep, long, shaking pull, and once again, degrade myself to myself. Damn!

… But today, I try another tactic; I ask a God I do not know to help me.

I have no business asking you anything. I don't talk to you. I don't bother you with requests or prayers. I'm not even certain you exist. But I hate that I smoke. It fills me with a self-loathing I don't even know how to describe. Look, so here's the deal. What if I don't smoke and you make it happen? That's right. I'm telling you I will not pick up a cigarette, but you've got to make it happen. I don't know if you entertain such requests, but I'm desperate here. If you parted the Red Sea, I imagine you can, if you want, keep me from picking up my next cigarette. So there it is. I know. Pitiful. I'm all screwed up. I don't even know if you bother to hear people like me. But starting right now, that's the deal. Okay?

I know people quit smoking on their own, all the time. But this was me, and I couldn't.

Who did I think I was, throwing out this presumptuous challenge to God? But he chose to honor my request. It's now thirty-four years later, and I haven't smoked a cigarette since.

Awakening: *Willpower can never defeat or resolve the sins that entangle me.*

December 23, 1979

I'm lacing up my New Balance 620s. I've recently started running. I stopped smoking three days ago.

Suddenly, conversation with God starts with one inaudible, but loudly perceived word:

Now.

It's my impetus to move forward. I have no idea into what. I only know it's time to tell God what I now believe.

In the last few weeks I've thought about where it would happen—the moment I'd tell him I'm all in. Should I go into a church? Maybe I'd go up Camelback Mountain and shout it into the night air. Now the moment has come and I'm sitting on a thrift store mattress in this dingy, bare, lonely guesthouse, which floods every time it rains. It's the perfect place to represent the end of things. The end of my running from him, the end of self-protection, of self-destruction, the end of fear, of pretending to be the victim of what I have mostly caused.

Awakening: *I am never more authentically real than that moment I ask God in. It must overwhelm him to have his love finally received.*

God, it's John. … I am so sorry. It's taken me so long. You've had to watch me go into so many strange and sad places. I want to do this right. I want it to take. Today, finally, no part of me is holding out. I have no other game plan. I am destroyed if you will not have me.

I want you to be my God. I believe you stayed on that cross for me, John Lynch. Somehow what you did was enough to make me clean if I believe it.

Today, I believe it.

Forgive me now. Jesus, for everything. It feels so wrong to ask you this. But you say that's what you want me to ask. I believe you were put on a cross and you allowed it, for me. You died for all my sedition; all my selfishness, all my rebellion and sickness. … Yes, I finally now believe you were raised from the dead.

I don't know what else to say.

… Except this. Why would you do this for me? Why would you let me care, why would you accept me after all I have done against you?

I don't want to become someone fake or pretend. But I'll do anything, go anywhere you want me. All I know is I want you, Jesus Christ. Wherever you are, you're the one I want. No one else. I'm calling this out loud for everyone in the universe to hear. This is John Lynch.

It probably wasn't as eloquent or well thought through. It was probably only a few sentences. But that's the best I can remember it.

John, pretty much that's how I remember it also.

December 1979

For weeks, I could barely catch my breath—as though I was could feel the synapses being rewired throughout my very being. Every moment felt supernatural and filled with endless, spiritual meaning. I was electric, pulsing with the experience of new life. I felt like I could walk up to someone in a department store and say, "You sir, fall down on your knees and trust Jesus!"

… and he would.

Over Christmas vacation, I now devoured the Bible, nearly every waking hour.

I wish there were some way to go back and experience all of it again. But I can't. No one can step into the same river twice. No one can feel brand new again. No one can repeat the first moment of worship. No one can enter from death into new life but once.

I know it doesn't happen that way for everyone. I wonder if God knew I needed a jolt to show me he was greater, more powerful than the drugs I'd taken, to overwhelm me. What God was doing for those days turned into weeks, made acid trips seem watered down.

I was so innocently looking for him in every moment, every verse, every promise. I read the section in Matthew about the rich young ruler. Jesus tested his sincerity by asking him to give up all his possessions to those in need.

So I did it.

I gave away my car to one of my students. I got rid of all my possessions except for a few clothes, books, cooking utensils, and several other basics. I sent checks to anyone I could remember borrowing money from. I nearly returned a dictionary and some masking tape I'd packed from my classroom when I left teaching.

I was naïve. For sure I was immature. I was probably butchering Scripture and yanking it into whatever I wanted it to say. But there was something so incredibly liberating about not yet knowing better. To run to obey God, not because I feared I would get in trouble, or because I was trying to assuage something, but because I would not miss any part of receiving God's love in full, wide open obedience. That was no mistake.

John, it was in those moments you knew you had believed. You were done holding onto anything. You weren't trying to prove anything to me. You only wanted everything with me. You didn't want to miss a thing. Yes, you were, say, a bit loose with the Scriptures. But I'm not complaining.

1980

So, what happened? I wish I could isolate the moment. All I know is this: nobody did it to me. I pulled the bait and switch.

I think I presumed every day would be that intense, that jaw-dropping. I imagined I was one of the last humans to be rescued and now the end would come. The boat door was about to close. All I wanted to do was ride across the country on a ten-speed, with a sleeping bag and a daypack, to coffee shops, telling everyone to get on board, because the show was about to end. John Lynch had become a Christian!

But weeks passed and I was still here. Slowly I realized I could still be sad, and I was not impervious to people cutting me off in traffic. I discovered my reactions and wrong affections had not been healed. I was experiencing stupidly immoral thoughts.

I would tell Jesus, "Don't listen to that thought. Please, I didn't mean it."

Then my thinking moved to this:

Of course! I knew I'd screw this up. God goes to all the work of bringing me to him and now I've got him disappointed. I do this to everyone. They all eventually leave. It's who I am. Damn!
… See, now I'm swearing!

But I knew I could not live without what I had found. I would not lose it. In that moment, like smoke under a door, it crept back in. Shame.

Awakening: *Increased devotion and diligence will not make me feel close to God again. Believing his never-changing affection will renew my joy.*

I guess I thought to get back feeling close to God it would take the same methods which once gave me applause and success: increased willpower, diligence, ought, berating myself to care more. That lie would spread its tentacles through my soul for many, many years.

It took so little time from first trusting him to arrive here: **"The second part of my life I spent trying to make myself worthy of the love I had found."**

I guess I could have challenged the lie.

Hey wait. Hold on. I didn't earn this love from God. I didn't figure this thing out. I didn't do anything heroic to get it. It was entirely one way. He invaded my destruction. Nothing I'm experiencing suggests he's one to bless me with happiness or withhold it by the constancy of my devotion. He knows me. He knew I was smoking three packs a day, dropping cheap acid and lying on my resume that I'd done standup comedy in L.A.

I wonder what would have happened if I'd simply called out to God:

> *Hey, I'm scared. I don't know what to do. I feel like I'm messing things up. I've spent the entire last week hiding from you, trying to figure out some formula to make it right—to make you happy with me again. I don't even know what I'm doing. I'm confused. ... And maybe disappointed. Is it all right to tell you that? I wanted it to always be like those first few weeks. Anyway, I'm freaked out and feeling this old familiar sense—like someone is about to leave me again. Don't go away from me. I've waited for you all my life. Please. I have nowhere else to go now.*
>
> *If I can know you're there, that you're not angry or disgusted and this is the way it's going to be, I'm totally good. I just need to know I haven't screwed this whole thing up. I'd like a sign or something right now. But I have an idea you probably don't often do magic when you're trying to form faith. That sounded like I know what I'm talking about. I don't. It's something I heard someone say. Then I repeat it and make it sound like me. I do that. I make crap up. Anyway, I love you so much. I can't make it go away if I wanted to. Help.*
>
> *Love,*
> *John*

... But I didn't do that.

My fear of losing this ecstatic experience of him drowned out such logic. I almost didn't care whether he operated out of peevish, manipulative jealousy or not. I wanted the feeling back.

When compelled, I don't know many humans more self-restrictively disciplined towards a goal than me. So I reared back and spent my best effort trying to find a way to get God to be pleased with me.

Awakening: *Nothing deadens us more than learning to perform from duty and ought, what we once did as the natural response of a new heart.*

... And my joy walked back into the shadows.

I didn't talk to anyone about it. Nobody told me they were doing a similar thing. But I soon found it was an unspoken way of life in most faith communities. No matter how much we sang of his unconditional love and sovereign power, we trusted more in our ability to keep ourselves in good stead. We were becoming religiously self-righteous and increasingly miserable.

1981

After several months, it became increasingly apparent Jesus was not going to time his return to my new faith. A friend, who'd been watching me devour the Bible, told me,

"There's this place where people talk about God and the Scriptures all day long, every day."

"You're kidding me! Where is this place?"

"They call it seminary."

"I must go to this seminary place you speak of."

So I left my teaching job and headed to Talbot seminary in California, driving another VW Bug. My boss gave it to me. I spent a thousand of my three-thousand-dollar teaching retirement to get it running. I poured a quart of oil into her almost twice a week.

I left Arizona with enough money to cover part of a semester of classes. How did I think I was going to pay for four years of full-time classes in a Masters program for which I had zero background? I guess I hadn't yet experienced a time yet where God had not met my needs the way I thought he should. I thought it was part of this new supernatural life. If I I'm attempting something right, why wouldn't he absolutely provide?

Arriving at seminary, I was a longhaired hippie with very little understanding of any Christian language or culture. I spent the first few nights in the parking lot studying my Hebrew declensions with a flashlight in my car. Learning a new language, especially one that reads backwards, was overwhelming and otherworldly, after a decade of aggressively burning brain cells.

Within several weeks I found a part-time job at a private Christian afterschool program. It paid me enough to afford a dumpy shared apartment, where Campus Crusade wrestlers routinely left lasagna-covered frying pans in the shower. I fished a mattress out of the apartment's storage. It had a large hole in one corner. Cockroaches were emerging from it. This was definitely a low point in my housing timeline.

After several weeks, the owner of the school took me to lunch.

"John, we're so pleased with the work you're doing at our school. Would you consider coming on as a fulltime teacher?"

"I'm honored, but I don't think I should. I came out here to go to seminary. I left my world back in Phoenix. I'm convinced God wants me in seminary. I know me. If I start working full time I'd never get through seminary. I left teaching to do something with God's Word. It doesn't feel right to have moved out here to do what I already left. I'm so sorry. It's a kind and generous offer."

I lived with the faith, and probably some presumption, God would get the money figured out somehow. I think God kindly chose to cover the absurdly grandiose checks I was writing.

A week later the owner of the school took me to lunch again.

"So, how are you paying for your seminary degree?"

"I'm using money left from my teaching retirement."

"How much?"

"All of it. Enough to pay for this first quarter."

"How are you paying for next quarter? It comes up in about two weeks, doesn't it?"

"Yes, it does. I don't quite yet know what will happen. I'm guess I'm trusting God will take care of me."

He got quiet for a while, soaking his fries in the au jus from his French Dip sandwich.

"Well, I also think God has you here to be in seminary. If you'd let us, my wife and I would like to pay for your entire time in seminary. Your books, insurance and all of your tuition. I'd only hope you'd consider working in the afternoon program as long as your studies allow you to."

I remember being incredibly grateful and excited beyond words that God had revealed how I was going to do seminary. But I was not astonished.

… This section was not supposed to spill out this way. Writing it is convicting me of a way of life I once knew and now teach about knowing.

Trust.

It wasn't presumption. I'd sensed real conviction from a real, actively communicating God that I should go to seminary. He knew all along how he was going to do it. I was convinced he knew. I can't remember the last time I knew with such conviction.

I'm sorry. I want to present a steady, gradually maturing man, released by the truths of grace. The truth is I often believed better back then than I do now. I can live now in much clutching fear of the future. I can think about positioning and covering bases more than trusting. I'm not quite sure what to do with this. It doesn't fit a clean narrative arch. It doesn't build a compelling argument. If I'm truthful, much of my life conflicts with what I know to be true.

John, you are not nearly as confident that I'll come through as you were back then. In fairness, I have done many things, allowed many things, did not stop many things you thought I should, would, must. It has rocked your world. It is hard for me to watch you scuff at the pavement, trying to figure me out, trying to reconcile my goodness with your pain and broken expectations.

I cannot let you write and speak continually about me without your authenticity being tested. Otherwise, your words will degenerate into untested and powerless slogans.

What you are teaching is largely true. But you do not always live it or believe it magnificently. Humans don't mature in a straight line. You and I are in a love relationship. These days, you've been hurt, confused, and devastated at what I would allow into your world. You are grieving. I know you do not always trust me. I am not angry or disappointed with you when you doubt my ways. I am only proud you would admit it here. If you want validation your life is working splendidly, you'll find it in your admission two paragraphs back. You're not nearly as good a liar as you once were. ...

1982

I am now living with two married couples in Santa Fe Springs. They are friends from my church back in Phoenix.

One spring evening, for the first time, I see it. Who I risk becoming—a higher-educated, striving, religious Pharisee. I see the life I'm forming, living out the implications of trying to please God by enough fervent effort and self-denial.

I'm in my bedroom, trying to pray. They are in the living room watching an inane television show. It's turned up too loud. Sitcom television sounds even more garish from another room.

My friends sound like drunks in a roomful of drunks. ... They are wheezing in laughter. I will one day wish I could be back with them in that moment, wheezing along with them. But at this time I am trying so hard to prove I am cut from different cloth. That I am more sold out, more passionate, more faithful, more attentive to God. Godly people do not fritter their time away in noisy and cheap laughter.

Only later will I discover I'm only attempting to disprove what my shame wants to convince me—that I'm not *enough*. I'm tied up tight in chains of performance. I'm judging my friends in the other room as halfhearted Laodiceans, not caring enough to be fully used by God.

Whatever I'm doing over the next hour is anything but prayer. I'm filled with seething, arrogant, religiosity. I'm babbling through a list I know I should care about, but don't.

God is out watching television, laughing with my friends.

At some point, I whisper out in a muffled scream: "I don't get you. I'm trying so hard to do things right and you don't show up! Those people are out there not caring about the things of

God and they're having a great time. Listen to them! Me, I'm miserable. I hate this. I'm watching the clock, every minute, trying to put in an hour, like those famous saints who said if they didn't get in two hours of prayer, the day was wasted."

Many of us face a time where we are tempted to blame God for not doing enough in us, fast enough, impressively enough. We become weary from doing all the things to impress him, expecting more return. "I'm trying, God. I'm trying! Help me. Tell me what you want me to do. I want to be a godly man. I want to do great things. I want to get over the garbage in me. Why don't you make it happen? I'm doing everything I know how to do."

This is actually a very good moment; when pride can turn into humility.

John, I wish you could walk out there and be with your friends. At this moment, they are throwing cornbread at each other and watching reruns of Mannix. I was out there with them, moments ago. So, this is an important moment. You are growing weary of trying to figure out how to please me. You've been trying so hard for so long. There is endless difference between straining for my favor by doing enough right and allowing my Spirit to draw out the good you now actually want to do. You are using your same old willpower and discipline to do behaviors you think I would want. Tonight you are witnessing the sham of your own performing. You're less than three years into your faith and completely miserable. I never wanted that for you. Have you forgotten how astonishing those first few months were? You were free, alive, and we talked like lifelong friends. Then you got religious on me.

So, you had to wear yourself out. Now you're becoming open to a new living out this faith in me. This is where it will start to get fun.

Awakening: *Many try so hard to become godly instead of trusting they already are.*

1983

"I've heard all about you. It just seems like a guy like you and girl like me should go out."

She's flirting with me! No one has flirted with me in a long, long time. I'm in Phoenix for a friend's wedding. And this unguarded, funny, attractive woman is playing me like a cheap banjo!

Stacey Marie Pilger.

I've seen her before. I've stared at her during services at Open Door, where my high-school students brought me when I first risked to enter a church. She's captivating. She's beautiful.

She will have little memory of that evening. I'm only a guy she doesn't know. What does she have to lose? She's so full of spontaneous, unrehearsed, unfettered fun. I leave her presence undone. Whatever smitten is, I am—stumbling to my car like a smiling, drunken man.

The next day I'm at a reception for close friends and relatives of the bride and groom. I'm in the backyard talking to the groom's grandmother. Not out of kindness, but because she's not getting up anytime soon. She is a safe place for me to hide out among strangers.

Stacey walks into the backyard and notices me.

God quickly goes to work in my behalf. God directly speaks words to her.

"That man, right there. He is going to be your husband. Go talk to him."

All afternoon, we flit around each other, like geeky junior-high kids at a school dance.

The next morning in church, she notices me staring at her. She composes a note and slips it into my shirt pocket after the service. It starts with these words:

"Blue-eyed one. I've noticed you …" The wonderful, soaring note ends with her phone number. I find a mirror to see if I have blue eyes.

… I'm toast. Toast.

Stacey says God gave her me to open up a life of significance, of grace—with children raised in tenderness, experiencing the immediacy of Jesus.

God gave me Stacey as my object lesson of my newfound theology of grace. All other women before her loved me *because* or *if.* Two decades of women told me they loved me. I think they did. Until they saw how messed up I was. My weaknesses, my fear, my irrational outbursts of panic eventually caused them to leave. When I was no longer the life of the party, they left the party.

Stacey is the first to love me just because. When I'm not on my game, when my breath is bad, in my pajamas with oily hair. When she sees the obsessiveness, insecurity, and jealousy in me. She is the first woman to convince me that who I am when I am not on is more than enough. Her love has shaped me more than any other person on this planet.

I get lost in lies that can still keep me from the truth of who Christ is in me. I can write and speak about the truths I love so much better than I can live them. So God gave me a woman who refuses to believe the lies I tell myself, whose playfulness draws me out from my head.

I always feared something horrible would happen to our world—that Stacey would go south, drift away in bitterness. In truth, when things do go south for us, it's Stacey who holds us together.

I will write this into my phone, on the patio of a restaurant at Crystal Cove, at our twenty-eighth anniversary dinner:

Today, twenty-eight years ago, we both took this high-stakes gamble that the other would stay in the arena. That day, she couldn't be sure, she didn't know if I would revert back to my old life, my checking out into isolation, medicating and running to the next place. She didn't know if I'd continue to allow Jesus in, to be everything for me, for us, and whatever family he would give us. I didn't know if she would be courageous, if she would stay in the hard times, if she would be faithful to me, if she would keep trusting him when it seems like he's forgotten about her. You don't know what the other will do. You think you know. You fall in love and hope.

But we put so much on the line, in those vows–trusting God to protect us, trusting the other to show up each day, even after we've failed or been adrift for so long. I don't know why we're still here, deeply in love with each other, in a deeply hard period. Why us? Many don't make it. They are not less good, less loving, or less trusting of God. I only know he is good and has been good to us. Beyond that, I'm not sure I can explain anything. But I do know this: after having seen the very worst life can throw at us, I'd choose her over every single woman in history ... save for Ruth from the Old Testament. I've said it before; I would have dumped Stacey early on for that woman. Stacey would have pushed me off a pier for a chance to marry the patriarch Joseph. But having missed out on those two, we've done all right settling for each other. I'm in for twenty-eight more. Then I'm out of here. Mark it.

June 3, 1985

The Sunday before our wedding, I was invited to speak at Open Door Fellowship. It was overwhelming to speak to the community who took me in during the first year of my faith. I prepared a message out of chapter three of Zechariah—my exegetical passage for my second-year Hebrew class. The passage presents a vision of the pre-incarnate Jesus defending Joshua, the postexilic leader of Israel. The evil one was the accusing prosecuting attorney. God the Father was the judge in the case. It's one of those wild and woolly Old Testament sections convincing me God must like rock and roll. There are forty ways to tell this truth, but God went creative and acted some of the stuff out, with others, in a dream sequence!

If there is a supremely important passage of grace in the Old Testament, this is it. Satan was accusing Israel of failing to be a defensible witness to God. "Joshua was clothed with filthy garments and standing before the angel." Satan knew if he could discredit him, the entire line of the Messiah would unravel. In the middle of the accusations, "the angel of the Lord" spoke. Whenever the article "the" (rather than "an") is in front of "angel of the Lord" in the Old Testament, most scholars agree we are watching a pre-incarnate appearance of Jesus. Wow! He rebuked Satan, and then turned to Joshua and in one sentence handed out the freedom from guilt he would one day purchase. "Remove the filthy garments from him. ... See, I have taken your iniquity away from you and will clothe you with festal robes."

I'm not sure I will ever spend forty minutes doing more of what I was put on this earth to do. I was frenetically working my way around the stage as if in that vision's very courtroom. Absolutely locked in the moment, I was having so much fun, I didn't want it to end. I didn't want to top out on one of my first messages, when I had several thousand left to go! But I think that's the case.

Stacey and I were in Lake Tahoe on our honeymoon, when we got word that Bill Thrall, the pastor who started Open Door, said these words the following Sunday:

"That was the finest message ever preached in this church."

The man who spoke those words had been the primary preacher in this church. In that instant, I knew I was a preacher.

At 3:45 a.m. twenty-eight years later, several thousand messages into this craft, I would write these words about what I have stumbled into:

Early Sunday morning is the most surreal four hours for some who preach. You get up in the middle of the night because you alone know the sum total of your study during the week has given you pages of sincerely good notes, clever turns of phrase and skilled segues, but no real message from God to man. So once again you panic and begin to beg God to show up. The ideas which sounded clever and insightful days before now barely hold even your interest. You ask God to give you something at the last second which would give something to someone. Life. Something to convince you that you're not bluffing this morning.

And then it happens. New thoughts, channels of entry, my heart engaged, courage to type dangerous, unrehearsed thoughts, vulnerability and ... slowly something like the very heart of God. That entire mechanically correct but hollow message I was willing, last evening, to foist upon a congregation, transforms in front of my very eyes. I've lost interest in whether it's clever or eloquent. For the first time all week, I'm believing what I will now preach. For twenty-eight years I've woken up before bakers and newspaper carriers, gambling God would do this. I wish he'd do it on Wednesday or Thursday, but he doesn't. And now, sitting in the dark with a cup of coffee, he did it again. No one may even notice the difference. But I will. It has kept me from feeling like paid clergy these last twenty-eight years. So, now I'm off to perform this high-wire act. I'm asking he'll turn this message into what he'd like for the one who risks walking over from the cheap apartments across the street, fearing God no longer hears her or wants to live through her. ... How did I get this privilege?

July 1985

We returned to Los Angeles, married. I excitedly handed a tape of my Zechariah message to the pastor of the church I'd been attending during seminary. I wanted him to be proud of me. He listened to it and passed it on to the head of the district in the denomination I expected to candidate for as I prepared to graduate.

Several weeks later he called me to meet for breakfast. A venerable and soft-spoken, white-haired man, he was deeply beloved and respected within the denomination. He'd been in this role for decades.

Have you ever had that experience where everything in front of you suddenly morphs into a slow motion crash, with the sound of screeching metal giving way to explosions?

His response to my message shocked my very being. The wreck was formed of these words:

"John, I listened to your message. What I heard was immature, self-seeking and self-serving. It was too dramatic and emotional. I tried to finish it, but couldn't. My recommendation is you not go into the ministry for quite awhile. Take some time to grow up, maybe volunteering with the youth at this church after you graduate. Preaching is a very serious and sacred endeavor. You did not treat it with the gravity it demands. That message was unacceptable. It offended me on many levels. Here's your tape back."

I have no idea what happened next.

I vaguely remember crying the entire way up the 605 from Long Beach to Whittier.

I don't think I've ever since worked on a message as hard as I had on that one. I truly believed it was the best I could ever hope to do, with a message allowing me to be the most fully John Lynch, representing God's heart.

All my life, I'd doubted my own sincerity. Only these last several years in Christ was I beginning to believe I could trust my authenticity was growing. Now here was a venerable religious authority questioning not only my capacity but also my character and motives. Everything was on the line in this moment. I would either allow someone to protect me or I would secretly bluff and pretend I believe my identity in Christ, when I no longer did.

It was so hard to tell Stacey. I feared even she'd change her perception of me. I feared the same when I called Bill. I was frozen. I didn't know how to move forward. "If I am wrong about that which I felt singularly most proud of and convinced of, then what do I know about me?"

Bill listened patiently to the entire story over the phone. After silence, he said,

"Well, I'm no prophet, but it appears this man did not enjoy the message or your presentation of it." He started laughing. I laughed too.

"John, maybe you do need to mature. Maybe a lot. But no one should take the permission to critique and rebuke another unless they're willing to draw closer into the solution. If you want, when you graduate, you could come to Open Door. I would commit to work with you on the issues of your maturing as much as you would like."

I'd been already candidating for church staff roles. One church in Oxnard had offered me a position as a "Christian Education Curriculum Director." One should probably not accept a job with a title whose meaning one does not understand.

"Look, John, this man's critique has forced you to form a conclusion about who you are. There are many people who can do a number of things well. You are not one of them. But many have spoken to me about the message you preached here. I have not many times experienced the presence of God in the Word like I did that day. You're a preacher, John. You may be young in the faith and immature in your experience, but if you can be convinced to stop speaking, many in the future will lose out. I can't think of a worse thing for you to do than to find a Christian job so you can have a religious title. Give me the phone number of those people who want you to be their curriculum director. They're making a horrible mistake. You'd be terrible at it. John, I'd be honored to help you get started speaking at camps and retreats and conferences. You could speak at our midweek service, to get some experience."

"You'd do that?"

"To keep those poor folks from having you as their curriculum director, I'd do a lot."

On that day, I experienced protection. Without it, I imagine walking around crippled, wounded and self-doubting; one of the best theologically trained shoe repairman in town. Without his commitment to me, to stand with me in the middle of my fear, insecurity and immaturity, I wouldn't have made it. I wonder how many thousands of hopeful young God-lovers have been sideswiped, without a Bill Thrall to brace them.

Two years later, in his backyard: "So, I think it's time for you to take the pulpit. I'll stay and help develop leaders. You're the one who should be leading us in the pulpit."

Something amazing happens when we stumble into spiritual safety. Many of us have never known it. We aren't even sure it exists. We've existed in the realm of "following Jesus" in a culture of being more right, accurate, and exact about our theological positions. We can go from theological conviction to creed to manifesto. But we're still on our guard.

Awakening: *We can hold the most orthodox positions, with exacting accuracy, and still be a lousy parent, unwise boss, or a board member no one wants to be near.*

All the while we convince ourselves we've put our ladder up against the right wall. But at night, it may occur to us ... "I don't know how to let my guard down. And I have a suspicion I make others all around me feel less safe."

Awakening: *Safety allows me to ask questions I can't when I'm proving myself. It allows me to trust another to describe me to me.*

1987

I told you when I was eleven I felt God.

I felt something that night I don't know how to describe. I don't talk to anyone about it. But I never felt anything like it before. I want life to be that way, the way it was those two minutes. I want it to come back so much.

Tonight I will see the best picture yet of what I felt that night.

Stacey and I are sitting smack-dab in the middle section of the prestigious Grady Gammage Theater in Tempe. We've been given tickets to see a new production of *Les Misérables*. I know Victor Hugo is a famous historic author. In Laguna Beach there is an elegant restaurant along the Pacific Coast Highway bearing his name. But I've never read this book. I know nothing of what we are in for.

My disdain for much that passes as musical theater is well documented. So, when the overture begins, I'm ready to endure an evening of over-emoted, vapid spectacle.

… But it is free … and the seats are great. … Bring it on, affected, garish vanity. Bring it on!

Then the scene with the priest and Jean Valjean explodes upon me. Suddenly the entire world around me recedes. I am alone, staring at the cold, thin, blue light enveloping these two.

You may know the story. A priest takes in a desperate Jean Valjean after his release from prison. He is repaid by having his silverware stolen. The priest discovers Valjean in the middle of the robbery. Valjean knocks the priest down and runs off. The next day, the authorities return a captured Valjean to face the priest.

What will happen next appears certain. Frightened, old priests want their safety, their silverware and uncomplicated justice and order.

But this is a real priest … who understands power.

He knows no rehabilitation or restraint will change him. Jean Valjean is convinced he is only anger, revenge, victim, survivor—a just man turned hard by injustice. Love is foolish weakness to him.

The priest knows he is infused with God. Love is his identity. He is made to love the unlovely. He became a priest not for a title and privilege, but to give dignity to those who don't yet know who they are meant to be.

Only one power will change Jean Valjean from the inside out.

Love, wearing the cloak of grace.

Sometimes old and feeble releases the most potent measure of brave and good.

... So the moment arrives. The authorities await the answer, which will send Valjean back to prison for the rest of his life. The priest has seconds to form his plan. He has already made his decision moments after he was knocked to the floor. Seconds are all he needs. Mature lovers don't have to weigh each moment. Their inclination to a response of love has been formed in advance. It is instinctual. Words not unlike these follow.

The lieutenant laughs, "He claims you gave him this silverware."

"Well, why yes. Of course I did. But, my friend, I don't understand why you didn't take the candlesticks. They're worth over two thousand francs. Why did you leave them? ... Did you forget to take them?"

The priest asks his assistant to bring the candlesticks from the house. The priest then personally places the candlesticks into the rucksack carrying the stolen silverware. The lieutenant orders the captive to be unshackled. The priest excuses the soldiers with the offer of wine inside.

He then draws close, so close, to Jean Valjean. He whispers, "And don't forget ... don't ever forget. You've promised to become a new man."

Jean Valjean responds, "Promise? Why are you doing this?"

"Jean Valjean, you no longer belong to evil. With this silver, I bought your soul. I've ransomed you from fear and hatred. And now I give you back to God."

How can this be? How will such a confounding, upside-down, utterly undeserved act of apparently foolish grace and mercy do anything?

How can Valjean see anything but a foolish, irrelevant old priest standing before him? How can anything ever change? Valjean is still who he believes he is. A hardened, skulking outcast, who must destroy to not be destroyed. Won't he soon steal again, only to be arrested again ... only to have everything he has believed about himself validated once again?

Ah, except for the power of love! More powerful than hatred and shame. More powerful than the course of the world, the pattern of humans, the way of things. More powerful than who we falsely believe we are.

The priest has played a well-worn card. For long before this day, he has understood his own hidden failures, his own duplicity, his own secret demons. And he has understood the unfathomable love of God, who calls him clean, beloved, and free.

This old priest stands and stares sternly into this man's face. He is speaking to the new man who will soon believe and emerge. He is calling to him with deep and solemn gravity. It is a voice and a strength which will haunt Jean Valjean until he obeys it. Then it will free him into a new identity, a new name, a new life.

When the grace and love of Christ are seen clearly they do not elicit a response of callous indifference or self-entitlement. They don't cause us to make sin less sinful, or breaking God's heart less bothersome.

It absolutely shatters our way of being. It either destroys the arrogance of our false piety or it strips bare the pretended enjoyment of our unbelief.

At first, we don't experience grace as tender and comforting. It comes to destroy the old fortress. We don't experience love as fulfilling and desired. It comes to rip apart fear and unbelief.

Once we see its unyielding demand, once we submit to its power and all-encompassing life, we become free. Freedom we have never even considered. ... In a moment, it changes the entire playing field and fills our hearts with dreams and pulsing life.

... Here, in the dark of this theater, I am watching what I was feeling that night as a boy. My eyes are filling with tears. Already, by eleven, I had learned to survive, to mistrust, to manipulate, to play all who wanted to love me.

I am no longer watching a play. I am being transported back to my childhood—to the night God revealed himself on my frightening walk home. The words the priest speaks to Jean Valjean mirror the impression God flooded my heart with, all those years ago:

John, you are marked now. You will run as fast as you can, but you will not be able to escape. You belong to me. You were made for a life of grace and redemption and love. Of freedom beyond what you can imagine. You have been bought. You just don't know it yet. And that feeling of being understood and adored by one who knows everything about you? It will lead you eventually home. You called me. I answered. I rescued you. I revealed me to you. It has filled you with a longing you never knew you had. Run, my friend. But know you have been marked.

And now, this radical, inscrutable, life-giving grace will now become my singular life purpose. I must find pictures, stories, and ways in—to allow others to experience this grace. Nothing else will matter to me. I will preach the grace of God, I will model the grace of God, I will live fused with God, the sustainer of grace. I will stand as an old priest in front of other Valjeans and I will "speak to that new man who will believe and emerge." I will fail at it, misrepresent it, and misapply it. But God will override every failure, and create beauty I had never imagined to see.

1988

I stumbled into a community of grace while wildly theologically opposed to the concept. I didn't learn this way of life in seminary. These young believers at Open Door Fellowship probably didn't even know they were influencing me so strongly. They didn't even know how to cogently articulate what was happening to them! But I watched them live with each other so well. It all got through to me.

For two years I was preaching to them all I knew: a "man-up," "buck-up" pile of theological-sounding self-importance and parroted platitudes. They endured it. I was boldly proclaiming a moralistic sin-management doctrine, while hiding the pain of my own compromise and immaturity.

It happens all the time, almost everywhere. We have a gift and it finds us a platform. We fall in love with being important. People actually think we know what we're talking about. The greatest drive is to keep our platform, because people start to admire us.

So we create a pretend, competent, assured self, hoping to buy ourselves some time. But it makes us less healthy and less teachable. They don't know we're lying. God still is growing them up in spite of our carefully polished mush. So a gifted, clever, funny, articulate young preacher blusters and poses as having a maturity and wisdom he does not actually possess.

Looking back, I can't understand why they didn't stop me. It's like they had a meeting. "Anyone else notice this kid is bluffing? Maybe if we stay close, eventually he'll catch on we're not buying his line. He may let us in. Then we get to watch the kid mature into these truths. Either way, he's still pretty funny."

So a community gradually teaches a preacher what to preach.

Awakening: *It's exceedingly difficult for anyone to understand grace as anything other than a theological position, unless they experience it in community.*

I remember the Sunday it happened. Some call it a "grace awakening." Bruce McNicol calls it "meeting Jesus for the first time, all over again." For months, I'd been studying Ephesians and been rocked by Paul's overwhelming account of what Christ has completed in us already. He's teaching the only way to live is to trust who we are in Christ and who Christ is in us. He's pleading we try no other method to face our sin and failures. I'm arguing with Paul all week before preaching this passage, "…be renewed in the spirit of your mind and put on the new self, which in the likeness of God has been created in righteousness and holiness of the truth." I keep rereading Romans 7 and 8, Philippians 3:9, 2 Corinthians 5:21 and Galatians 2:20. They are forming a chorus convincing me I'm a saint who still has sin but is adored, rather than a saved sinner who is a grave disappointment to God.

"Yeah, but what about personal responsibility? What about fighting the good fight? What about living with fear and trembling?" For so long those verses appeared to demand a buck-up response. Now they are slamming up against this new conviction of a Christ who had already radically changed me and is now maturing me in his perfect timing.

A friend recently gave me a copy of Brennan Manning's *The Ragamuffin Gospel.* Manning is destroying me with his ragged and brutal admission of his pretense, arrogance, and pretending. He is building a case for trusting only in Christ's power in him and the unwillingness of God to receive even my own condemnation. He is exposing my charade.

This Sunday morning's message begins with an apology:

"Something is happening inside me. I've been bluffing to you, trying to impress you with my seminary insights and knowledge of the original languages. I actually don't know enough of either to understand what I'm talking about. I've talked tough and told you to be sold out to God. The truth is, I'm not doing this life very well. I'm in a continual battle of willpower against sin. I'm losing, badly. I have no idea how to communicate what I am beginning to understand about living out of a new identity. It's still pretty elusive to me. I'm sorry it has taken me this long. I only know I am tired of forcing this Bible to say what I think it should say. I've wanted it to tell you off, so I could get you people to be better. It has been ugly and humbling to realize I'm the one who doesn't know how to be better. That's all I've got right now."

God sets me on a course that morning to discover how to articulate this way of life in Christ. This time it will not be in isolation, but in a community learning it together.

Jesus has been waiting for me to start reading the Word without a shame and moralistic filter. Only then could I understand him saying this to me:

You and I are absolutely and completely now fused with each other. Your strength, joy, hope, peace, everything will come from risking this to be true. We are melded as precious metals. Yes, I am God and you are human. But the unthinkable has happened. All of me infused into all of you. It is impossible to discern where I begin and you end. I am no longer God up there with you down here. I am now closer than a burning bush, a vision, or even a Peter sitting next to me. I am now identified by you my dear friend.

Your true identity is Christ in you. You may absolutely put your entire weight upon this. It most perfectly honors what the cross and the resurrection accomplished. Please don't shy from this in some religious sense of it being too good to be true or beyond your worth. This declares your worth. Enjoy this with all your being. Don't waste a day pretending it is not true. I promise you it is.

Awakening: *We're all screwed up. Only bad religion can cause us to pretend we're not. We're still compromised and maturing, even on our best day. It's just better to know we are.*

1990

I almost peed my pants, right in front of my audience.

I was in the middle of an illustration on a Sunday morning. All of us started laughing and couldn't stop. It was one of those times where you think you'll stop laughing and then somebody in the audience snorts and you're all back on the train.

At one point, I stood there and stared out upon this congregation with tears of laughter in my eyes. I was struggling to catch my breath.

It's like we were speaking words behind our laughter to each other:

Audience: "John, we never thought we'd get to be like this in a church. It's incredibly exhilarating. But do you think God likes that we're playing around right now? This story you're telling—it has no point, no value. It's like a lead guitar solo in a spiritual song. We want to believe our God values all of this. But it does seem sort of wrong."

Me: "I hope he's delighted. I'm banking everything he's in it all. That he enjoys it all. That it's all part of this incredible being he's remade us to be. If we're in him, it's all God stuff. This enjoyment, it too is created by him! I have a feeling he's laughing as hard as we are."

Audience: "We were hoping you'd say that."

Awakening: *God is not afraid to risk the consequences of what we do with his grace.*

I could have landed in ten thousand other communities, where there would have been a built-in religious expectation I would've had to fake my way through. To be in a place that was risking to trust I am Christ in me felt so freeing and dangerous all at the same time. We're trusting we have new hearts that can be trusted. We're trusting God with the pace of each other's maturity, humor, and kindness. And many of us are getting healed in the gamble. ...

Awakening: *One of the most freeing moments in my life is to discover that who I am as a Christian and who I really am have become the same person.*

1990

Back in 1983, Mike McDevitt and I were watching a rerun of the sixties television show Bonanza while we ate lunch in the home I shared with the McDevitts and several others.

Long story short: "Little Joe" Cartwright was the handsome son of Ben Cartwright. Ben was the wise, kind, and benevolent patriarch of this wealthy ranching family. This particular episode ended with the two of them working through a breakup with a young woman Little Joe had been seeing. Little Joe was sad.

Ben was about to make a final, concluding, profound statement. It's what he did. He was a strong man of few words, but the ones he chose carried immense weight and should be heeded by his children. He put his hand on Little Joe's shoulder and said these words, which apparently would make sense of all the heartache Little Joe was facing. It was the last moment before the episode ended and the theme music started up.

What both Mike and I heard was this exact phrase: "Bubbleen, Little Joe. Bubbleen."

I looked over at Mike. "Uh…did he just say…?" Mike answered, "Bubbleen." He said "Bubbleen, Little Joe. Bubbleen."

Me: "That's what I heard! He can't have said 'Bubbleen'! It means nothing."

Mike: "I think his exact words were 'Bubbleen, Little Joe. Bubbleen.'"

There was no rewinding in those days. Unless you worked as a film editor at the network station, one shot was all the consumer got.

We must have laughed for twenty minutes about "Bubbleen." There's no other phrase it could have been! We substituted dozens of alternatives, trying to give them the benefit of the doubt. But nothing worked. What important phrase of help from Ben to Little Joe could possibly rhyme with "Bubbleen"?

"Break my spleen, Little Joe. Break my spleen."

"My real name is Lorne Greene, Little Joe. Lorne Greene." "Bub, we're on the big screen, Little Joe. On the big screen." "Boy you're lean, Little Joe. Boy, you're lean."

"Let's get out of this scene, Little Joe. Let's get out of this scene." Nothing fits it.

Six months after that I moved and wouldn't see Mike much at all for nine years. But I told the "Bubbleen" story dozens and dozens of times to friends, wherever I went. I shared it when I've taught at conferences and camps. I used it as an illustration in a Sunday morning message. Maybe I've been hoping someone can shed some light on it and put this mystery to bed.

My relatively new friend, Bob Ryan, has heard me tell this story in different settings many times already. He is a freelance graphic designer and is teaming with a local design artist on a magazine project.

Bob calls me. "John, I'm working with a guy named Mike McDevitt. Could this be the Mike McDevitt from the 'Bubbleen' story? He's a design artist in town."

"Wow! I didn't know Mike was in town. Yes, that's probably him!" Bob says only this, before he hangs up: "I've got an idea."

... It is now four days later. Bob's meeting with Mike again. They are standing over a large, angled, design board. The project paper is in front of them and they are trying to solve an issue of design space usage. Mike is a bit frustrated he hasn't found a solution yet.

Then God releases the hounds of humor. Both men are standing over the document. Bob taps his mechanical pencil on the table and says these words: "You know Mike, this puzzle we're trying to solve is sort of like 'Bubbleen, Little Joe.'"

... And then the three seconds of wonder I can barely wait to see in heaven. I will ask to see it over and over and over again.

Mike turns his head, as on a swivel, leans into Bob, and exaggeratedly mouths, slowly and sternly, "What ... did ... you ... say?"

Mike has not heard these words from outside his own head since 1983. His expression conveys that if Bob does not say the exact words in response, Mike will choke him until he does.

Bob, in a moment of near genius says this: "Yeah, 'Bubbleen, Little Joe.' You know, from the *Bonanza* show. It's a statement people make when they hear something which doesn't make sense. You hear people in graphic arts use it all the time. It's like saying you've got a conundrum or a paradox of misunderstanding. You know, 'Bubbleen, Little Joe.'"

Mike stares at Bob like he has said, "vegetable mallet of corrosive steam harnessing."

Mike: (moments of staring, then attempts to form words without success) "What?"

Bob: "'Bubbleen, Little Joe.' Come on, you know. Ben's trying to help Little Joe. And no one can figure out what he says next. Stop screwing with me. Now, let's get back at this."

Mike: (more trying to form words without success) "Where did you hear this? How do you know this? Nobody knows this. There's only one other person who ..."

Then, mercifully, Bob smiles and says, "I know Lynch."

Awakening: *God is able to stand in the pain and injustice, while at once transcending it. He employs humor, which reminds evil it cannot win.*

1991

All my Christian life I haven't known what to do with my sin. I fought so hard against it. But I rarely saw significant change. Now I'm married. I'm discovering I can hurt Stacey in so many ways. I am still very frightened to have my unvarnished self presented in public. I'm still a frightened performer. I want to be perceived a certain way. Stacey cares nothing about such varnish. She has no supreme court. She usually says what she thinks, without working the angles. This now includes talking about me. I make her pay whenever she speaks of me in a way I don't like. She is losing herself more and more under my control. I don't know what I hate more than hurting Stacey. She has little agenda, little guile. She is being Stacey—trusting God to convict her on her error in his time. She understands grace, most of the time, better than her husband, who is endlessly preaching it.

I need to discover something stronger against my sin than self-loathing and stronger promises. Only a community can try out and prove this truth:

Awakening: *Trying to fix me won't help. But if I don't have to hide, my life issues will begin to be resolved.*

What will protect Stacey is the courage to tell on myself as quickly as I discover wrong.

Awakening: *The courage to tell on myself about the wrong I am intending to do is one of the most heroic actions I can take.*

To tell on ourselves before we do the action is a stunning display of the new life in us. We are choosing to no longer give ourselves permission to do something that moments we were willing to risk integrity and health to gain.

Such a choice is revolutionarily supernatural. It also happens to be the only thing we can do to stop sin once it begins to present itself to our consciousness. No self-discipline, no intense striving, no promises, no beating ourselves up, no other anything will stop sin's power once it forms. Any other means than telling another is so utterly pitiful. We are trying to resist a failure we've already given ourselves permission to do! The very action of resistance only heightens the anticipated pleasure of the acting out.

As certain as dawn, when I choose to tell another what I am planning to do, it breaks the cycle of sin's power in that very moment. This is why we're asked to confess our stuff to each other. Even stuff that hasn't yet happened. Because the inflamed darkness brewing inside is only waiting for time, location and opportunity.

Imagine! Having a friend safe enough to call and say, "Hey, it's John. I haven't done anything yet. But I need to talk to you, because I trust you. You need to know what I'm plotting."

In that moment, we are free. Free!

It will come again. But this episode has lost its power. For this is the grace of God offered in real time, for real life. He is not out there; he is in here, at the most crucial moment.

Awakening: *The objective is not to build communities appearing to have sin under control. The objective is to nurture a place safe enough where people can stop faking they have sin under control.*

It's messy but utterly healthy. Those who live in it become free ... and they end up sinning less.

A true leader is able to stand in the tension of such a community, even such a work environment. There will always be structure, expectations, and something worth doing being done with great diligence. Many leaders never learn the best environment for great accomplishment is an environment of trust, safety, and authenticity. Any other means of accomplishing anything eventually misses the quality of relationship needed to remember why we were doing the work in the first place.

Awakening: *If you gain permission into my life I will allow you to stand with me to challenge the lies I tell myself.*

It's here where the real work of healing and freedom is proven, not in the moment I am about to act out.

To be given such permission ... there is no higher calling. It breaks the self-entitlement I give myself to fail. It protects my wife ... and everyone who crosses my path.

1993

This August evening I'm in the audience at a mission conference in town. I've been told the speaker is a very inspiring, gifted and influential luminary, being powerfully used all over the world. I'm told I'll like him a lot—that we are a lot alike.

From the moment the guy starts speaking I want to walk up to him and punch him in the larynx ... over and over, until he's willing to stop speaking. He's manipulating an audience with passionate, idealized stories, and cheap emotional appeals to be more for Jesus. It's all filled with comparison, guilt, shame, and contrived sacrifice, couched in a pitiful manipulation of

mangled verses. I'm scanning the audience, to see if others are ready to join me in harming him. Instead, I can quickly tell folks are mesmerized with him, hanging on his every oily word.

I shake myself and dive back in—asking God to calm me down and forgive my rush to judgment. But I'm not buying my own prayer. Why doesn't someone stop him? I force myself to stay in my seat the entire talk, hoping the look of incredulity on my face will trip him up a bit. But he's on a roll. I could light myself with a blowtorch and he's going to finish.

After the talk, I'm pacing through the hotel like an angry ferret. Another pastor stops me, staring wide-eyed at me like he's just heard Lincoln give the Gettysburg Address.

"Was that the most inspiring talk you've ever heard, or what!" I'm definitely thinking, "or what."

The halls are buzzing with excitement and accolade.

I find a stall in a bathroom, far down the hall from everyone.

God, what was that? Are you with his message? Everyone here seems to be. These are leaders. I'm angry. I want this to stop. But his message is powerful. It's what people want to hear. It appeals to their sense of wanting to be the most sold-out they can be. He's yelling compellingly to everyone's shame and ought. And like lemmings, they're all buying it. I didn't come to you for this! I feel all alone again, like I'm on the outside. Like there's a Christianity I still don't belong to. Do you want me to feel this way, or do you want me to go back inside and nod my head? I can't fake it again. I won't fake it again. Help me. I'm officially freaked out here.

From this moment I know, while I might have the same Jesus with most believers, God has been directing me into an entirely different way of living with him. For seven years I haven't been aware how wide the gap was.

For the next twenty years I will battle to defend what I believe is the Original Good News. I will try to do this without being consumed by disdain for any human purporting a manmade sufficiency doctrine of the flesh. I will fail at this, too often. But I am now inexorably drawn to authors, speakers, and thinkers who are risking to see grace as far more than only justification.

1995

The set is now completely appointed for *Cappenetti's,* our next production, set in a local bar. It's magnificent! The warm wooden counter top, and overhead racks of wine glasses, framed by vintage looking columns, fill nearly the entire back of the stage. Neon beer signs hum, while diffused light from a series of ellipsoidal reflectors spills down through the rack slats. Every conceivable libation is backlit prominently from behind where the bartenders will pour. Taverns in big-city gaslight districts wish they were this place.

We open in two nights. "We" are a theater troupe named Sharkey Productions. We have been painstakingly learning how to write and perform faith-based stories for the city that don't offend sensibilities by bad writing and religious right turns. It might be an easier endeavor for monkeys to type out *The Old Man and the Sea.*

We've written a number of fairly mediocre plays our first several years, but recently we're starting to find our footing.

The several dozen of us committed to this dream are having the time of our lives. For the first time, I'm discovering close up an intimate place where I am known, enjoyed, and needed. We laugh more than we rehearse, and we rehearse a lot. It's an immensely safe place to create and risk and fail and create again. We love being together and are starting to learn to protect each other. This is one the most enjoyable things I've ever done.

Several years from now we will be performing at the downtown prestigious Herberger Theater. But now we are performing out of our church. We've remodeled the auditorium to look like a cool retro theater.

The crisis doesn't dawn on me until the Sunday before we open. I'm sitting at church thinking, "Five days from now this stage will transform into a neighborhood tavern." This would be a marvelous thought when we only staged the plays for one weekend. But for the first time we are running *two* weekends. The set, complete with every imaginable alcohol and blaring beer sign will be the decoration for our church services the following Sunday.

I know it's no big deal anymore. But at the time it was. Knowing what I know now about how this community sees community, faith, and buildings, I wouldn't have panicked. But I was still testing it all out, to see if it could be real. I'd now been on staff for nearly five years. But this project is my deal. I'd tried to not give anyone reason to have issue with what we were doing. Now I'm asking first-time visitors and alcoholics to show up and take communion in front of a fully functioning bar!

Sitting there, my issues with authority flood back in: all the doubt, all the waiting rebellion. I'm certain we'll have to tear it down and reconstruct it. I could ask if we could drape it with canvas. No, that's stupid and weird.

Finally, I went to Bill.

"Yea," he said. "I was thinking the same thing today. You won't be offended if I don't preach from behind the counter, will you?"

"What?"

"Look, this is a building. On Sundays many of us who show up are probably God followers. On Fridays and Saturday many might not be. God is happy to host both. It's a building. We don't violate anything by doing both. If sometimes the décor blurs together, I think folks will understand. If not, maybe we can help teach them or thank them for their time here. You're not covering that majestic set. We're so proud of you all. You're us. You represent us. I can't wait for opening night. I can't wait for the following Sunday. With our crowd, your biggest concern is people trying to sneak off with a shot of the good scotch after the service."

In those words, something ends in me. From this day on, I am never again waiting for the other shoe to drop. The sense I don't belong. That who I am won't fit in any church. It goes away. In that moment, I know when I fail, I won't be asked to leave. I know I will not have to eventually run. Ten thousand questions are answered with one response.

Awakening: *We grow up wanting to be known, and terrified we will be.*

1995

I'm sitting in one of many repurposed military huts at the Gasinci Refugee Camp in northern Bosnia. It's a sticky June afternoon. Two brothers and their wives are slowly and quietly recounting for us the particular atrocities of the hell which has fallen upon Croatia, Serbia, and Bosnia these last half-dozen years. None of them make any noticeable facial expressions. They speak in monotone. It is an eerie and heartbreaking experience to hear the one brother tell, without any emotion, of their third brother having his throat slit.

Everyone has walked with a suitcase or grocery bag many miles, through and around enemy checkpoints, to end up in this camp. We are the latest in a steady stream of well-intentioned caregivers to these war-displaced families. Every person we meet can tell of a family member killed, tortured, or raped in this hideous ethnic genocide. No government is innocent, but most of these refugees are. They didn't want this war or cause this war. And now their own neighbors, with whom they have loved and done life, suddenly are enemies—burning homes and torturing old friends. A sick appeal to religious differences, national unity, and ethnic cleansing has demanded such.

I am worn down. This is our third day in the camp. Every story blends together. We're here to offer the hope of Jesus. But they are so wounded, so devastated, so full of shock and thinly buried rage, the offer of Jesus must sound like the promise of free accordion lessons.

"What you are offering might be nice in some other world, but right now we are waiting news of how many family members are still alive and if we will be allowed to stay here another day."

I feel cheap. Listening to these couples, I realize I have come here with exceedingly wrong motives. I wanted to do something relevant and big for God. I wanted to go where there was the greatest need. I wanted to be in the center of the action. I wanted to have stories to tell of walking among the wounded in a war-torn country. I wanted to be the hip pastor who would go into harm's way. I wanted to come back home to our church with a report of the dozens who trusted Jesus.

Yesterday I listened to a man who had watched his entire family cruelly killed, back home in Banja Luka. After listening to his story for awhile, I tried to offer him the hope of Jesus. He shook his head slowly, back and forth. Through an interpreter, he said these words:

"What do you want from me? I have lost my family. Where is God? And who is this new God you are trying to sell me? I don't want a God who would allow what I have seen. What do you want me to do? Would you like me to pray a prayer, so you can check off a list back home? I will do that. I did it for the last group. If I do it, would you then please leave me alone?"

I was embarrassed for the interpreter. I was embarrassed for me. I excused myself and walked out of his barrack.

God, I want to go back home. I don't want to do this anymore. I don't like who I have tried to be—the great American caring Christian. Help me. I don't know what to do. I have no relief gifts to offer. And you apparently are not what they are looking for at this moment. I don't know how to help. I feel trite and useless. Nothing seems strong or supernatural. It's like you aren't here. I hate this feeling. I'm so sorry to write these words. I know you are here, but I have never felt oppression and darkness like I have these days. Help me fill the hours and get through this until we get on the bus taking us to the airport on Friday. I'm sorry I came here. I'm sorry I can't do anything. I'm sorry I'm misrepresenting you.

I wander around the camp until early evening, when we all get into the van, back to the seminary in Osijek, Croatia, where we sleep. Others are loudly recounting stories of hope and spiritual openness. I have nothing.

It is now Thursday morning. We make the drive back to the camp. I am making the rounds to yet unvisited refugees, with others, keeping a low profile. But it is too much to take.

I break from the group again to go outside and wander the camp. I notice down in low-lying areas some even worse conditions. Apparently, even in refugee camps there are the haves and have-nots. I am informed this is where the "Roma" stay. The Roma are the present-day Gypsies who still live throughout Europe and the Balkans. I watch a deeply wrinkled older man making impressive, intricate wooden spoons and vials. I offer to buy some. He is so appreciative. Eventually I am asked into his family's "home." It is a stagnant, hot, dark room with no windows. The air is thick and full of sickness. A large hunk of indefinable meat sits on a table, flies devouring it. I so do not want to get sick. I want to excuse myself. But a man, perhaps in his late thirties calls out to me. He is seated across the room, cross-legged, on the dirt floor.

"You are from America, yes? So, why are you here?" He is clearly the leader of this family.

"Well, we're here to, um, offer comfort and, um, spiritual help to the people who have been through so much sadness."

"You're here to talk about Jesus, aren't you?"

"Well, um, yes. But we want to be sensitive to those who are not, um ..."

"Tell me about this Jesus. Would you to be so kind?"

For the next hour we both talk and question and answer, and ask some more. The room begins to fill. They are leaning in and listening intently. I am suddenly willing to contract whatever is in this room. For the first time on this trip I feel like Christ in John, being me. I am falling in love with humans from another continent.

When it's over, he asks if he too can be a Christian. He asks me what he must do. I lead him through a rough, clumsy talk he could have with God about trusting what Jesus did at the cross and the resurrection. He prays it out loud in front of everyone. Then he gets up and hugs me.

He is smiling and so kind. ... He offers me the meat on the table. He sees my hesitancy, and we all laugh. Others hug me. Jesus is fully here. He was here the other days. I couldn't see him, in the middle of my straining to prove myself.

"Why was this so different?" I asked myself on the ride home. Maybe it was this:

Who I am, Christ in me, wants most to love. More than anything else. That's the real me.

Awakening: *I am a lover on my worst day and misplace it only when I pretend I have what I'm not sure I do.*

I heard later he was baptized by someone in the group following us.

... Someday, at a wedding feast, in a land far away, we will meet again. And he will not be living in the bad part of town. He will be right in the middle of the city lit with the glory of God himself.

1997

In most of my preaching, I don't usually give anyone anything specific to do with it.

Others can do it skillfully and naturally, but I usually feel manipulative or hokey. I guess I've always thought God could direct people to do whatever he wanted them to do with what they were being taught. It's a nice-sounding theory, but in practice it's a bit ridiculous. All areas of learning involve and include practical application. Jesus did it with his own teaching. I haven't known how to do it without coming off like a motivational speaker, selling soap in an ill-fitting shirt.

One Sunday I am speaking on 1 Peter 5:6–7: "Humble yourselves under the mighty hand of God, that He may exalt you at the proper time, casting all your anxiety on Him, because He cares for you."

"Casting your anxiety" has the idea of throwing a saddle over a horse, or hurling something with all your might. So I asked each family or individual to later try my clever little *action step.*

"Find a pillow case and gather your family around your dirty-clothes basket. Have each of them think of something that creates anxiety or frightens them. Have them pull out an item of dirty clothing to represent that anxiety. Spend some time teaching how God is able and longing to take it away if they cast it onto him. Give each person a chance to tell their particular anxiety. Then let each person stuff their dirty clothes item into the pillow case. Tie off the top and take your whole group out into your front or back yard. Take turns casting the pillowcase. Come back in to express what it was like throwing your scary thing into God's care."

… My seminary preaching professor would have been so proud of me.

By the time the morning messages have been delivered, I've lost interest in the whole exercise. But people will be expecting some kind of report about our family time the following Sunday. So I have to try it out at home. I have three children to try it out on. Carly is four, Amy nine, and Caleb eleven.

Late one afternoon, I gather us around the dirty-clothes basket in our bedroom. I have to admit, it goes really well and it's a lot of fun. We're all into it. We laugh and talk about our fears, and pray together. But, at the end of the day, I'm mostly going through the motions, trying to host a God moment for my kids.

I'd forgotten all about it by the time I went in to lie down with Carly before bed. Twenty minutes later I kiss her goodnight. Before I step out of her room, my little girl calls out:

"Dad?"

"Yeah?" "They're gone."

"What do you mean? Who's gone?"

"The monsters. The ones who lived under my bed. The dirty clothes I put in that bag for Jesus to help me with. They're gone, Dad."

I'm overcome in the doorway of her room. "Carly, that's incredible."

The hall light streaming into her darkened room allows her to see only my silhouette. She can't see my expression. I'm wrecked. I'm witnessing God interacting with the trust of a human. My little girl has not yet learned to not trust God. She believed he would do something, sometime. She believed he had her back. He did. I know not everything plays out like this. But it shook me. Trust in his power, his rightness, his ability, his love, his control over every moment of my life—it's not an option for us. Not at the start of the journey or any day after.

Carly spoke of the monsters often before that day. She never speaks of them again.

In this moment, I am compelled to believe again what I've forgotten. Somehow, in all the perfect, sovereign plan of God, some experience the magic of God because they trust him to be able to do it. It freaks me out, but it's what he appears to promise. On this day, preacher man misses it, but his four-year-old daughter gets it. She still gets it.

John, you can get information or knowledge from anyone, without almost anything on your part. But to receive wisdom, insight, discernment, or truth–ah, that will take trust. One can come simply through the brain. The other demands the heart's buy-in. To the extent you come under my words, trust my way of seeing, you will become wise. All around you are intelligent and knowledgeable people imagining they are wise. But they are only educated with what can prove them more right than someone else. They lack humility to trust another.

I will never fail you or play you. Come under my assessment, even when you don't understand or like it. You'll become wise. You have been hurt in these last few years. It has left you disillusioned and self-protective. This guardedness of your heart will leave you dry. If you don't let me in, the wounded man will face his pain without wisdom and insight. This will create an even deeper pain.

John, allow your daughter to teach you tonight. This is no longer a preacher's gimmick. This is supernatural life, my dear friend.

I will become convinced that wisdom is the inevitable response to this:

- Trusting who Christ says I am, even when I don't feel worthy of it
- Trusting who Christ says he is, even when he doesn't appear to be active in my experience
- Trusting others with me, to protect me from my self-referencing madness
- Trusting his Word, even when it doesn't portray the way I think God should be

1997

It's so crowded at Squaw Peak Park this Saturday morning, I have to drive all the way to the top of the loop to find a parking spot. The peak itself is a steep, switch-backed hike, embedded with jagged rocks for me to trip over—to become the lead story on the five o'clock news.

"Hello, this is Kent Dana with Channel 10 News. Today, an elderly, dehydrated hiker plunged down the western slope of Squaw Peak. In what took several hours, because of his fragile condition, paramedics eventually airlifted him out. Witnesses at the scene said he looked nearly incoherent before hurling headlong down the steep, cactus-strewn slope. We'll update you on his condition in a special report at ten."

I hate this hike. It offends me on so many levels. It shouts at me, "Hey, old timer! I'm going to make you so miserable. I'm going to make you question your manhood. ...You're out of shape. You shouldn't be here. In the first quarter mile we're going almost straight up. You'll be gulping for oxygen like you're on the moon. Little children will be passing you. You'll slug down your entire bottle of water before midpoint. And you'll create a rash from wearing Levis. Did you think you were going to hike a furniture store?"

But Stacey wants to hike it, so we are here. I am now walking down from the parking lot above. I dropped her off at the trail head, nearly half a mile down the same hill I will have to retrace later—after I am left dehydrated, rubbery-legged, and belittled by nature. I am in a bad mood as I wander around in my head. At such times my head is a rough neighborhood.

I am complaining a steady internal whine. My whine is interrupted by this random thought: *My golf game is so bad I'll bet I could shank my drive from the Biltmore golf course into this park.*

The course is over a mile from where I'm walking. But self-pity knows no distances.

Maybe fifteen steps after that thought, I look down. There, directly in front of me, mostly buried in the clay dirt ... is a golf ball!

And I am suddenly overcome.

There it is again. That Presence. That overwhelming sense of him. That invading and overarching experience of being gratefully swallowed in awe.

I kneel down to pick up the ball. It is covered in the mud of last week's storm. I clean it off the best I can. It is suddenly an iconic, visible, tangible expression of God's ability to meet me at any single moment. This ball is from him, saying,

John, I am here. Last month, a boy grabbed one of his father's golf balls from the backseat of his family's car, from the same parking lot where your car sits. He rolled it down the hill and lost interest in it as it rolled across the road into this culvert, where you now stand. I not only let him decide to lose interest, I formed that random thought for you and directed your eyes down at the exact moment. Pretty cool, huh?

I am undone and lost in whatever worship is. In this moment there is no pretense or overreaching words. I can't speak. I am standing for several minutes, holding this ball, not willing to leave this moment with my God.

I find Stacey and tell her about what just happened. She gives me that slight head tilt that says, *My husband is a bit of a kook.* But I drive directly home after this walk, wash the ball off, write the date on it, and place it on my office shelf. For the rest of my life it will stay with me and remind me, draw me, hold me. I am yet not aware much is heading towards me that will bring nearly everything into question. But today, I am given this. I have this ball. Others have the Shroud of Turin, or nails from an ark. But I've got this golf ball from God himself.

Awakening: *God is not only out there, watching me. He is in here, fully identifying himself with me.*

He is doing this life with me; completely and uniquely living my experience. Love has gone this far.

1997

The first thirteen years on staff at Open Door, it almost felt like I was stealing money, receiving a paycheck. It was that fun, that incredibly life giving, that fulfilling. I read and hear of those who say no local churches can be trusted once they gain any significant size. That the Spirit of God will always get squelched by a system's power, agenda, and program. They are mostly correct. I know I would be on their team if I hadn't experienced those years at Open Door Fellowship. But I lived in it.

Early on, the life-giving safety and power and beauty of this community got me dreaming. I wanted this environment to be perpetuated all over the world. I could imagine a campus that would draw others to come and live in this clumsy but authentic community of grace. I could see it in full color. A center of art and drama, teaching, and interaction. A place to experience grace and life and learn how to read the Scriptures without a filter of moralism. A place to learn vulnerability, affirmation, and authentic friendships. A place to fail. A place to be released into dreams, destiny, and need. We would have a tape ministry, sending these truths of identity and grace all over the world. This message, this way of life, this life in God is that important. It simply must share the marketplace of ideas with the prevailing luminaries who peddle systems of earned spiritual maturity.

I naively thought we were impervious to the divisiveness and broken relationships so many other communities seemed to live as normal.

… Then the dream unraveled. Almost overnight.

I honestly still don't know what happened. To this day I'm still not sure how much my immaturity or inflexible kingdom building played into it. I'm still not sure why it had to happen. But it did.

In the course of the next year, our outreach to the neighborhood formed a church in a different location. Much of it was so good. But some of it carried wounding from some hurtful decisions of our leaders. I became estranged from one of my very best friends with whom I thought I'd do ministry for the rest of my life. Open Door moved into a temporary rented facility we could only use on Sundays. Friends began to leave. There was a growing spirit of mistrust over our community.

I tried everything I could do to keep it patched together. I couldn't believe others would be so willing to sacrifice this dream over what I considered lesser issues.

My heart got broken. And I fought against the loss with all my heart. But I couldn't help much anymore because I was losing objectivity. I was making myself the issue. And I was hurting others in the embarrassment of my immaturity.

I got revealed in all my stuff. I hid myself away.

And the fun completely stopped.

I was fighting so hard for a vision I was certain God was part of. That period of time taught me a life-giving truth:

Awakening: *God is infinitely less interested in my vision than he is with my person.*

Until authenticity and maturity and dependency are realized, my vision will be crippled.

Years went by with me learning nearly nothing. I was gritting it out. I still preached well-prepared and sincere messages, but my heart was frozen. I found it almost impossible to forgive the ones I was certain wronged me so grievously. The person key to my pain didn't even seem to be fazed by it all. He was thriving. Until he was willing to own his part, I was unwilling to even consider my part in all of this. I was trying so hard to hold on to my rightness, my vindication.

I began to blame God. Didn't he care? Couldn't he see this accurately? Did he have the power to defend me and rectify this dream that seemed to be quickly slipping away?

After a year or two, I gave up hope of it ever getting better. All I wanted now was to move on and be freed from this pain. To leave the rotting, embarrassing corpse of my dream. I received a preaching pastor offer from a church in Ohio. A few of their leaders heard me preach and offered me the job without having me candidate. It would give me an out. I was in so much pain, I called them back. Stacey told me I could take the job, but she would not be joining me. Our kids were vitally tied into our youth ministry. They had lifelong friends already. I couldn't leave. I was stuck. I was embarrassed. And I was miserable.

John, this is the saddest time in our relationship. To have to sit on my hands while I watch you lose hope in my ability to make wrong things right. I must watch you suffer in your pride.

I am not ignoring you. I am standing over you in the arena, so you cannot destroy yourself. Light is coming. You are tiring. I am here. If I thought there was a better way to bring your heart home, I would do it immediately.

John, here's what you don't know. You are going to stay. Twelve years from now you will still be an elder when the truths and environment you longed to see lived out will begin to thrive again. You also don't yet know I will spread it to places you've never even heard of. The ministry Bill and Bruce are developing will spread this message all over. You will do much of the writing for it. You'll speak in places you never imagined. I did it, John. I didn't do it in the way you thought I would. But I did it, I'm doing it and will continue to do it, until time runs out.

In these twelve years you're maturing into the man you always hoped you'd be. I've been doing that also.

Awakening: *God protects the humble but has to sit on his hands until the proud get weary enough of defending themselves.*

2001

I never wanted kids. They would get in the way of my dreams, my impact on the world. I wanted to be married to someone. Stacey only wanted kids. Apparently, I looked like I might be able to help provide her with kids. So she taught me how to love our children. Nothing since has been more important to me.

I know the absolute love of all three of my kids. They know only my accepting love and full commitment. I have given them each the best of me. They each play with me, make fun of me and listen to how I see life. They affirm my life like I could have never possibly imagined—in notes, in public, in birthday letters of overwhelming affirmation.

My friend Norm Wakefield says he loves each of his kids most. "Dad, do you love me most?" "Oh, yes. Absolutely. By far." He says the same to each of them. They get it.

Writing this, I love my youngest daughter Carly most. Amy and Caleb have fought with each other plenty growing up. But neither of them ever fought, argued, or got sideways with Carly. Who argues with someone kind, loving, and without much guile?

She will one day become our resident philosopher and biblical studies savant. She will already understand more theology, have read more books, and probably understand how to exegete a text better than me by the time she's twenty.

I fear her best days will have already been behind her. She peaked in this year. For she and I, over a nine-month period of time driving around in the car, have created songs filled with free association. I will never forget a single lyric of them. God has been gracious to give me a child who enjoys the bizarre non sequiter nearly as much as I.

Here's a sampling of the songs coming out of this season with my eight-year-old.

"The River Goat"
Hey, Hey, the River Goat, the River Goat's on our team.
The River Goat, The River Goat,
The River Goat's on our team.

"A Bucket of Squirrels"
A bucket of squirrels my friend is now.
A bucket of squirrels my friend is now.
A bucket of squirrels my friend is now,
He's not one to bake a cow.
A bucket of squirrels my friend is now.

"A Water Buffalo"
I wish I was a water buffalo,
I wish I was a water buffalo.
For if I was a water buffa,
I would be so very tougha,
I wish I was a water buffalo.

And this potential Broadway tune:

"Keplinger"
Keplinger, Keplinger, he's a mouse.
Keplinger, Keplinger, where's your house?
Keplinger, Keplinger, don't be a louse.
Oh, find your way in the–
Find you way in the–
Find your way in the world.

… Cholesterol plaque may now take me at any time. My work here is largely done.

2002

There are moments when God shows his hand. When they happen, I find myself apologizing for every moment I've doubted his character, plan, and love.

Tonight, my family is in Tucson, at the University of Arizona, watching Caleb run in the 800 meters in the Arizona high school state finals.

He has been a distance runner since seventh grade. But something changed late in this sophomore year. He started running the anchor on Washington High's 4x800 relays. The last four races, he's been running down some very good runners in the last lap. He actually qualifies at regionals to go to the state meet.

It's now an hour before race time. I am more nervous than when I ran at Camp Oaks. Caleb is not. He knows why he's running. He's not owned by what drove me. When I grow up, I want to be like my son Caleb. There is something so overwhelming and humbling to be a father who starts a line of faith in a family. I'm still stuck in a bunch of generational patterns my family line passed on. But now I'm watching my children, healthier than me, thriving because of the faith I've passed on to them.

I'm now bent over, behind the stadium bleachers, with a growing sense I may be momentarily throwing up my concession-stand nachos.

There's something about tonight that feels disproportionately important. It shouldn't. Caleb is a sophomore. He'll be running against some of his great heroes—legends of Arizona middle distance running. Matt Burton has already won State in this race before. It would be notable for Caleb not to finish last.

I start begging God. This is not prayer. It's a father's full-on, selfish begging.

> *Father, protect my son. I know he can't win, or even place, but let this be a heroic night for him, where he gets to see your hand.*
> *...*
> *Forget that! Do something supernatural. Let him find a way to stand on that podium. There I said it. I think I'm going to vomit.*
> *Wait. One more thing. My dad's here. He's starting to drift away with dementia. I would love for him to see Caleb run the race of his life. So, there. I'm begging. Don't let tonight hurt him. ... Being a father is so hard. I find myself caring more than I ever have and now absolutely unable to help.*
> *... Okay. I really am going to vomit now.*

At the starting line he looks like a boy lined up against full-grown men who've already financed their own homes. He's terribly thin. He fills out his uniform like a lizard wearing a suit coat.

... The race begins. Caleb's on the inside lane, and immediately gets boxed out. He looks passive, like he's frightened to be in such a field. He tries to make a move, but is quickly trapped inside. As he runs by us on the first lap he breaks free and rushes up on the pack. I've seen this before. He's started sprinting too early. His heart is bigger than his endurance. He's very fast, but can fade at the end if he gives too much too early. Predictably, on the backstretch, Matt Burton steps into another gear and bursts out to a twenty-yard lead.

... Then, on the backstretch, Caleb makes a decision to go after him. He gasps out:

"Okay, God, I think this is going to hurt—a lot. Thanks for getting me to this moment. Cover me. I'm going to make a move with all I've got. Here we go."

In moments, Caleb works his way through the pack and is actually making a move on this modern day centaur. No matter what happens now, even if he fades to the back of the pack, Caleb has broken a family-line pattern of fear. He has risked greatness and not pulled back into less painful safety.

By the final turn, he sprints up even with Burton. The stands erupt at this unexpected turn of events.

What was a coronation has now become a race.

It's hard to comprehend what I am seeing from my son! "What is he doing?"

I realize Caleb is not just trying to make the podium. He actually thinks he can win this!

This last stretch is where Burton has buried the hopes of dozens of very good runners. They're lulled into thinking they're in the race, and then he steadily pulls away, with his refined form and strong, long strides.

Caleb's form is starting to break down as he reaches deep for his final seventy yards. Accumulated lactic acid is surging through his body. He's visibly contorted and locking up.

...I've suffered this scene before. Caleb will fall short. We will all congratulate him afterwards on a great effort. But he will fall short. That's how life plays out for most of us.

But now, shockingly, with fifty yards to go, Caleb is still hanging on to him ... like a shredded flag in a hurricane.

Nearly everyone in the stadium is now standing. It's like they know the outcome, but want to honor the courage of both runners. It is thunderously loud around me. With twenty yards to go, this is no longer about who is the better, stronger runner. This is about something entirely other.

The last ten yards will be forever etched in my mind. He looks behind by at least a step. He's lunging more than running.

Caleb then displays what he has recently discovered, but has yet to risk in such competition: He has another gear.

Still twisted and gasping, he strides even with Burton. And with one more shockingly fast stride, he leans forward—

… *And hits the tape first.*

The crowd around me is wild with stunned delirium! Stacey, next to me, is moaning a crying yelp, blended with a guttural howling. I look over at her. We both are crying. I scan over to see my father. He's three rows in front of me. Instead of taking in all the whoopla in front of him, he turns back to stare at me. I have never before seen him make this openmouthed, stunned, ear-to-ear smile.

Late in the night, with everyone asleep in our Tucson hotel room, I lie in bed with our video camera propped on my chest. In the dark, I am watching the race over and over—to make sure it still actually happened.

John, there is funny and then there is you under those bleachers. One of the perks of my job is I get to see wonderful moments no one else does. And I get to create moments like that frozen stare between you and your father. That too, was prepared from before the world began. I have many more such moments coming. This life is hard. It will get harder. But my extravagant love does not begin in heaven. I love you in the now.

Oh, about Caleb. You know he wasn't supposed to win that race, right? Ninety nine times out of a hundred, he wouldn't have. But what he said to me on the backstretch; it overwhelmed me. I am undone at such daring trust.

2003

Bob Ryan and I are in Tempe this evening. With three hundred others, we are packed into a bar named Gibson's, waiting for the concert to begin. Bob and I have cowritten most of the scripts for Sharkey productions over these years. He's become one of my closest friends. He's the most gifted writer and song-writer I know. Brilliant, well-read, and exceedingly funny, he may understand Flannery O'Connor and Bob Dylan better than they understand themselves. In the seventies, his folk-rock band was being groomed for a contract with Asylum records, until drugs did him in before the band could make it into the studio. He can sing all the harmony parts to "49 Bye-Byes" and still writes and records exceptional music informed by that era.

He tells me the truth about my preaching. He has cared enough to call me out in my nonsense. He enjoys and understands my particular gifting as much as anyone I know. He has stayed close to me when I have run others off.

… And he is an absolute mess. He has lived for decades with a deep, abiding faith in Jesus and carrying a heavy backpack of compulsions, obsessions, and addictions. He represents millions. Maybe he represents all of us. I know there is an entire strain of Christendom which teaches such dissonance cannot exist in a "real" believer. But I will choose to walk with his deeply dependent faith over a crowded, shiny ship full of pietistically, self-managed strivers. So will God.

As a young pastor, with no small Messiah complex, I used to believe I could help "fix" Bob. I couldn't. I can't. Eventually, in some ways, he will probably be more of my teacher than I will be his. Bob has clumsily trusted God for any health he carries. Such is the astounding beauty given to those who stay in community long enough.

Awakening: *All untested religious answers get tested over time. Only what is from love remains.*

This is when the wisdom of dependence and humility begin to reign. Friends stop posturing and become real to each other.

He and I have gone through so much there is very little pretense anymore. Ten years from now, when I set out to write this book, it is his voice I will first need to hear. We will set aside several days and go north. We will be sitting on a cabin's deck, overlooking the forest surrounding Prescott. I will ask him what he thinks of my idea to write this book. He will puff slowly on his cigar and say:

"John, you're not nearly as good a writer as you are a speaker. When you speak, you have this supernatural God-presence thing. When you write … not so much. You will have to be you. Don't write to make a point you think you should. Don't bully people you disagree with. Sometimes, on your blogs, you go after an enemy I'm not even sure exists. Write what you want to write and only that. If you don't represent these truths with the natural, unforced story of your life by now, you probably haven't believed it anyway. Tell your story. Don't prove anything. Who knows? Maybe some of the stories will be salvageable to perform on the road. That's where you're best."

See what I mean?

Anyway, this evening, we are seeing Bruce Cockburn in concert. Bob introduced me to his music ten years ago. If I could see only one more concert before I leave the planet, it would still be Cockburn. He's a Canadian with a slightly better following than retired bull rider Bobo Gleason. He's spanned five decades, playing a combination of folk and rock which seems created exactly for me. He's angry, while profoundly and tenderly hopeful.

He's a God lover. You wouldn't catch it by much of his music. But some of the most transcendent words about Jesus I've ever heard were penned by him. For me, with few exceptions, those considered "Christian artists" carry some measure of synthesized feel to their music. I know that sounds smug and immature. But what Bob told me about writing is true about music. Those who aren't trying to prove anything prove the most. How many lines are better than "fascist architecture of my own design"? Or, "You tore me out of myself alive."

Cockburn will play this song in the next few minutes. He wrote it back in the eighties. I will stare—transfixed and closer than usual to my place in the universe. The song will be the anthem for the rest of my journey.

Fascist architecture of my own design
Too long been keeping my love confined
You tore me out of myself alive

Those fingers drawing out blood like sweat
While the magnificent façades crumble and burn
The billion facets of brilliant love
The billion facets of freedom turning in the light

Bloody nose and burning eyes
Raised in laughter to the skies
I've been in trouble but I'm okay
Been through the wringer but I'm okay
Walls are falling and I'm okay
Under the mercy and I'm okay

Gonna tell my old lady
Gonna tell my little girl
There isn't anything in the world
That can lock up my love again

2003

It's February 16. I'm sitting on a stool on the back patio at the Encanto restaurant in Cave Creek. Stacey has been planning this fiftieth birthday party a long time. I have chosen to celebrate my birthday by taking this occasion to list and describe the hundred greatest influencers of my life. Many of them sit around these tables.

It will be the last time I will have this large a gathering for a birthday. I am as much in the middle of community life as I will ever again be. I will be known much more outside my little world not long from now. But I don't yet realize how deeply I will miss this group, which will change and grow smaller over the next decade.

I've asked for there to be no affirmation time tonight. Such has been done for me, in astonishing measure these last twenty years, more than for anyone I know. My friends have each come with written notes that I will cry my way through before bed early in the morning. Tonight is to affirm them, to affirm our community, our way of life. I am in the middle of a predestined moment—to bless not only those at the tables but all who have been part of this improbable journey to grace. I am fully in the moment, fully made for this moment, fully apart of it, fully undone simply in the affirming these lives who have helped save my own.

Stacey has arranged for Steven Larson to share a hilarious piece he has written, mocking my every idiosyncrasy. He is one of my all-time favorite humans, and perhaps the funniest person I know. He won't let up. All of us are laughing like hyenas, filled with helium, gasping for breath.

At some point, a song is played. I look around the gathering and get lost in this thought:

> *You took this chameleon, who never felt known, and you let me be known. With no pretense, no props. These people have seen the worst and best of me. They value me, and allow me to influence them. How do I thank you for this? This evening feels about as good as this life will ever be able to give. You saw this too, didn't you? You put this together, with all my tastes, desires and favorite moments. You knew exactly what I'd want.*

|||||||||||||||||||||||

> *Drink it in kid. I'm sitting in the back, watching every moment. This is what I could see the evening Arlene broke up with you. You have no idea what your seventieth birthday will be like. Oops! Shared more than I probably should have. "Waiter, another glass of Syrah, please."*

2003

Amy and I are sitting in my car, up on the mountain again. Same pattern each time. I buy her a chocolate shake from Wendy's and we drive, north of Lincoln and Thirty-Second Street, until we are overlooking the city. I ask a few questions. She gives short, begrudging responses. We sit some more. When I realize it's not going anywhere, I drive us back down the hill. This is drive number six.

I'm not sure what else to do.

Amy's been hiding her life from us—going to bed when we do and then slipping out later to the computer, entering conversations she knows we'd fight her on. She's becoming more closed off. She's been fighting everyone's protection of her and hiding communications from a world she doesn't want us to know about. Now, she's pulled away. I never wanted this in my family. I thought I'd done everything to prevent it. I find myself going into "cop" mode, where I make ultimatums and threats of loss of privileges. I hate this. I never wanted to be that dad.

I think she's not opening up to me because she's not sure she can trust me. I've been pretty absent for awhile now, buried in my own aspirations. Amy pays the most of anyone for the absence of my emotional presence. She's forced to figure things out herself, to come to her own conclusions, formed in isolation.

I am only now seeing it. I'm desperately trying to earn my way back into a trust that can protect her heart. She wants it so much but does not want to be fooled again. She can't tell if my sudden attention is because I'm doing the good Christian dad thing, or because I adore her with everything in me.

Today's approach is different. I have no agenda. I want my daughter to know my sorrow, my apology, my commitment. I am tired of fighting her. I want back in, so badly. After a few minutes of silence, I blurt out:

"Amy, I don't know if you believe me yet. But I would give up everything I am or can do. I'd move our family to Grass Valley and deliver mail to convince you of my love. I don't have anyone in the world I love more. No one. I will do anything to convince you I want to be your fan, your protector, your hero. I will not lose you, my daughter. I'm so sorry I've been so self-consumed. You needed me, and I wasn't there. It will not happen again."

That day she melted. She believed me. She opened up and poured out her sadness. She let me back in. For the next year we will meet almost every week for coffee before school. We will go through Proverbs, 1 Peter, 2 Timothy, John. Mostly, we will talk—about everything and anything. She is listening to me in a way I have never been listened to. I am listening in a way I've not listened before. I am getting to be a father in a way my father longed for with me.

One afternoon, months later, I ask Amy for her keys so I can put her new registration form into her car's glove box. I open the door and there, taped all across her dash, are 3-by-5 cards, with verses and quotes from our times together. I stand, transfixed, at that dash for a long time. … My daughter has been drinking it all in all along. She is wanting to live out the life her father is trying to describe.

I come into the house, not knowing what to say. She's sitting on the couch, staring at her laptop. Had she thought about me seeing those cards when she gave me her keys? I choose to not say anything and she doesn't seem to be waiting for my response. I sit near my daughter, smiling, as I thumb through a magazine.

Awakening: *My children desperately need me to own my failures.*

… It allows them to trust me so they can express their own pain, vulnerability and best moments.

2004

"I'm going to do it this time. I'm going to quit. I'm quitting Truefaced. I'm not pretending." This has been the theme on my last thirty or so walks with Stacey. She knows me so well. Anymore, she nods her head and smiles, "That's nice, dear. Tell them I said hello."

Nobody's taking me seriously. But I will do it. I mean it.

It's been too much. If I don't take a stand, nobody's going to advocate for me. I'm working half-time at the church as the preacher and half-time with Bill and Bruce speaking and writing for Truefaced. Two halftime roles are turning out to be three fulltime roles.

I'm seething, feeling taken advantage of, not sufficiently appreciated. So I write up my resignation letter.

I've done this all my life. When things get hard or strange, I become a free agent and give myself permission to make all my decisions, in isolation. Then I move on, thinking I'm thriving for awhile—until the next conflict.

I call Bruce and ask for the two of them to meet with me. I say something cryptic like: "It's very important. It's about my future and stuff."

I walk into the room the next day to find them both at one end of the table. I sit at the far other end. Before anything can be said, I dramatically slide my letter of resignation toward them. Bruce picks it up and both of them study it with serious intent. They speak quietly for several moments. Then, Bruce looks up at me and says, "Bill and I categorically reject your resignation."

"What?" It takes a moment for me to process his words. "You can't. This is America. I can quit if I want. You can't reject it. It's not your call."

It gets quiet.

I glance up to see tears in Bill's eyes. He says, "Of course you can resign. And we could not stop you. … It's just … that I don't want to do this without you. I guess I thought when the time came it would be because we all had a chance to talk it through and agree it was the best thing. John, I'm intentionally tied to you. I committed myself to you. And I'm not sure what to do now."

It gets quiet again.

"Would it help if instead of giving us this letter, maybe you could let us hear what we've been doing to hurt you and maybe we could work together to correct it? You can quit at any time during the conversation. But we might be able to correct this and get to be together for a long time. Would you like that?"

"… Yes, I guess I'd like that."

It's what I wanted all along. It's what I'd wanted all my life. I'd just never found a place where such was possible.

Awakening: *When leaders stay long enough to work through pain, hurt, and disappointment, those who walk through their doors innately sense something real.*

That day we talk and listen, apologize, forgive, and playfully mock each other. Later, I tell God I want to never again unilaterally declare an independence from my commitment to either of them again.

I don't think I have sufficient words to describe what the commitment and friendship of those two men standing by me has meant to me, to my family, to the expression of everything I've longed to do with my life. The three of us, for many, many years have been trying out an experiment of faith tens of thousands are now risking, all over the world. We are believing we are better together. The power of us in relationship is truly more profound than what I can do alone. Giving a gospel of anything less misrepresents what God is after.

Awakening: *When we give another a safe and authentic place to be known in their failing, we protect them from true failure.*

John, this will not be the last time you run. You will try to run again. And again. But you have learned something today which will guide you and protect you for the rest of your life. You realized you are not a free agent. You have loved and are deeply loved. This love creates a responsibility and a commitment. You are no longer as free to run. You may all agree one day to disband ministering together. But you will not disband your friendships. You are no longer free to do life independently. You are no longer free to let expediency and opportunity run roughshod over commitments of love. This is much of what it means to be owned by love. It is what many have hoped for but not seen in action. As clumsily as you do it, it gives majestic hope to others watching it.

2008

It's been several weeks now since I returned from the eleventh annual "Ernest Borgnine Memorial Music Appreciation Society" weekend. A long way back, about fifteen of us, all good friends and addicted lovers of music, decided we would get together several times a year to share our favorite pieces with each other. We needed a name. Someone tossed Ernest's name into the mix. It seemed to fit. An actor, who's been in film and television for over half a century. I think we liked the name, and the fact he seemed to be such an affable, approachable personality. So, for over ten years we've been getting together, each of us usually arriving with CDs burned of thirty to forty-five minutes of music representing our lives.

To begin each event, we play the theme music from McHale's Navy while a giant smiling placard of Ernest sits in front of us. On our turn, we each usually give some introduction, explaining how we're doing, often including extensive printed packets of lyrics, pictures, artist biography, or our own written reflections on why we picked our particular music. It's a sacred and sometimes absurdly wild time. We pray for each other. Someone usually plays their own music. There's always great food, cigars, and a featured wine pairing by the resident bartender. During each man's "set," no one gets up or speaks much at all, respecting each other's offerings. Last year was the culmination.

Several got the idea of writing to Ernest and letting him know what we do. We knew we risked freaking him out—seventeen grown men playing music in front of a placard drawing of him.

But we thought it worth the risk.

He received the email and his agent communicated he'd be honored to see us. So, several of us flew out to his home in Beverly Hills. He was so touched that several months later he boarded a plane to join us for our tenth annual event!

We each included a song on a compilation CD we made for him, sharing why his unbridled joy and self-effacing ease made him the perfect fit for our yearly shindigs. One of us created artwork on the CD and on the matching t-shirts, bearing his smiling mug. He danced, laughed and sang to the music. I read a story of his life I had prepared. We listened to his stories about Lee Marvin and Betty Grable. He let us call our parents and he talked to them! It was a rare and marvelous weekend.

Late the first evening, he stunned us with these words: "Gentlemen, I've been honored all my life for what I've done. How incredible, at this stage of my life, for the very first time, among men half my age, I would be honored for who I am." He shook his head from side to side and then down. None of us spoke for a long while.

Awakening: *Affirmation heals and humbles and makes me want to do more of what I'm being affirmed for.*

On Sunday morning, after we each prayed for him, in front of him, he cried, and said, "If church was anything like this, I think I'd come all the time."

2009

I'm driving in my car with Joel Try. Though twenty years younger than me, he has become one of my closest friends. He is funny, incredibly insightful, and understands beer like I understand burying clothing.

I used to try to mentor younger people. I'm lousy at it. As soon as I call it that, it gets strange and I start trying to say profound things all the time. Everything becomes a spiritual metaphor: "You know, that bowl of baked beans reminds me how we can stay stuck in unforgiveness. Perfectly good beans mired in the muck of their own bitterness."

It's too much pressure for me, and a lot of work for the person I'm trying to mentor. Joel is the first younger friend I get to be John around. I'm trying to believe if I'm Christ in John, and I love Joel, then eventually something meaningful will happen. Even if we're drinking coffee together, telling each other the stuff of our lives. I'm sure this revelation won't make the feature article in *Discipleship Journal* but it's the only way I can do it.

Joel is going on and on about some young, hip, famous preacher and some hilarious, insightful story he told, from some best-selling book, in some amazing message, at some world-changing conference. For the sake of the story, let's call this guy Rob. After awhile, I begin feeling insecure. I snap out something about "not trusting the guy." "At some point Joel, you're going to have to decide if the stuff I'm telling you is opinion or counsel. You can't listen to everything and not own responsibility for where it's all going. Maybe it's time we stopped meeting."

It's crazy talk. I know it as soon as it's out of my mouth. I am being inflamed by the reality I am not that hip, famous preacher. Now it spills out, all over Joel.

Now what to do. I've blown it. We will never again be the same. I've sabotaged my influence with my fear. The mentor is the immature one.

It gets very quiet in the car for several minutes. When we get back to my office, neither of us gets out. We sit there, each unwilling to unsnap our seat belts.

"John, so, I don't know what that was all about. But you need to know I don't have anyone in my life I trust like I trust you. You've taught me a way of seeing life I never knew. So you kind of made a fool of yourself back there. I get that. But I swear to God, if you think you can leave me because you sometimes get weird, think again. Because I will make your life miserable. You're not walking away from me, Lynch. Do you hear me?"

His dad had checked out on him. For so long he'd been guarded against allowing anyone in. He's saying, "Don't you understand? I let you in! I don't need you to be right all the time, or even always more mature than me. I need you to stay. You don't get to run away from me. You taught me that. Love stays. It doesn't walk away because things get strained. I'm not going back to the hidden, untrusting guy again. Get over comparing yourself to that preacher. He's much cooler than you. He's smarter and he knows history better. It's not going to change."

Awakening: *Once another trusts you to influence them, you lose your permission to run—even when you don't feel worthy of their trust."*

Such a community gives you a chance to take off the idealized mask of the shaman. There, in all your rawness and unpolished compromise you are revealed as someone much more enjoyed, loved and trusted.

2010

Stacey and I awaken this morning in Santorini, Greece. A deeply generous couple has sent us on a once-in-a-lifetime trip for our twenty-fifth anniversary. How much we spend is of little issue to them. We've been gallivanting around the globe like wealthy retired people—from Paris, to Bordeaux, Venice, Tuscany, and now Greece. We took the hour-and-a-half gondola ride in Venice—just because we could.

This morning, we find ourselves sitting next to a Jewish couple in our elegant restaurant at our elegant hotel. The food is so good, I want to stuff cheese Danishes into my pockets. Over the next hour this couple is becoming our friends. We are invited to join them on a tall-sail dinner ship, which will drift from one white-bleached-building-covered island, to another, as the sun slowly paints the sky deep red. On the ship, we meet another Jewish couple. Within minutes we are all laughing and yakking, like we've known each other all our lives.

They want to know our story. I don't want to tell them. I don't want to ruin the evening and our friendship by telling them I'm a Christian speaker and writer. I've seen how this plays out. I usually sense it is my responsibility to make sure they hear the Gospel. I almost always feel like I'm selling soap to people who were moments before risking to trust me. They feel betrayed and confused. And I'm left with a bad taste in my mouth.

The couples persist. They must know all about us. After Stacey and I briefly explain our lives, they are full of questions. Not defensive questions. Honest and vulnerable ones.

In a moment, I decide to see where God takes this evening. I am a Christian. They know who I am. Tonight, I will not proselytize. I will love and be loved. I catch Stacey's eyes and realize she is good with taking a similar tack.

The next several hours are filled with life. We are having marvelous talks about everything: parenting, marriage, love, failure, regret, periodontics, books, my book, the Cleveland Indians. We are enjoying each other with such honest freedom.

The man from the couple we met at breakfast takes me aside.

"I almost always feel disrespected and devalued by Christians. Like I have no faith, or my faith is all wrong. I want to tell them, 'You know your guy is from our team, right?'... Anyway, you aren't doing that to me. Thank you. I know you're probably struggling with this, thinking you should be saying more. But I already know what you would say. I've heard the message from Christians so often. Here's something you may not know I see. Most of us see it; I know you Christians have something. I really do. I'm incredibly intrigued. You're giving me tonight a chance to test out what I'm seeing without being clubbed like a baby seal. Thank you."

Stacey and I had earlier decided when the ship docked we'd walk up the steep, ancient donkey path leading up from the sea to this cliff-carved town. The two couples had already decided to take a gondola to their hotel. We are half way up the path, pausing to watch the Mediterranean Sea reflect the moon. Then we hear voices. They are calling our names. It's our Jewish friends! They've run up the steep path to catch up with us. They are fully out of breath.

"Hey, we couldn't do it. We didn't want the night to end. We didn't want to stop seeing you. Would you guys let us buy you drinks? There's an outstanding bar at the top, overlooking an incredible view below. They serve the best Mojitos on this continent."

Within minutes we are sitting together in the bar, leaning back on comfortable cushions, overlooking lit pools and patios below us and the moon above us on this open-air pavilion. It is all majestic, serene, and otherworldly. The climb and the humidity have made us all desperately thirsty. I'm slurping down Mojitos like they were ice teas. I've never been in a moment where people with such radically differently faith are so honest about their doubts, wonders, and dreams of how we hope life turns out. In trying not to force the gospel, I've unwittingly given the gospel in a much more loving and comprehensive way than maybe I ever have.

It is now 2:45 a.m. I am officially drunk. I didn't mean to be. But I am. We all hug and make promises about vacations we will take together. Then my loopy chick and I maneuver our way through the streets and alleys of ancient Santorini, feeling very much like savvy locals.

The next morning I ask Stacey, "What happened last evening? Did you feel all right about our conversations? Even when they asked me directly, I didn't want to give them the formula. I wanted to let Christ love them through me. To allow myself to be loved by them. Part of me feels like I let God down for not closing some deal. But a much larger part of me feels good. We all need God. They don't need him more than me. Every day I need the redemption and healing of Jesus. I wanted them to know that. I guess I'm counting on this conversation continuing. But last night was so beautiful to me. I don't know when I've ever loved people who don't believe our faith, the way I get to love people who do."

The old order of John Lynch—pious, religious man—has been changing for a long time. But what happened last evening revealed it to me. People are not unwitting candidates for my speeches about God. They have profound dignity. They carry the image of God. God is sovereign. I know there may a time to explain more, but last night was not it. I think he likes it when I'm not manipulating conversations to get to the bonus question.

I'm three continents over, being taught by Jews how to be a Christian. Shalom.

2012

I remember holding Caleb as a baby thinking,

God, I'm counting on this way of life in grace to work for him. This feels like a huge risk. Am I right to raise him this way? I want him to grow up in such safety, freedom, and life that he will never have to rebel. I want him to know who he is in Jesus so strongly that his new nature will guide him to obedience, rather than religious compliance. I want him to never have to fake it, or pretend an expected life. I want him to know the power of God to mature him from the inside out. I want it all to be so real to him. I want him to be closer to God than I am.

Then came Amy ... and Carly. We were a family, trying out this way of life in grace. I was falling in love with being a dad. I watched Jesus make our faith real in front of our kids. Each of them were gradually coming to trust him on their own. It was hard to believe that this man who had run from God for so long was having the privilege to help raise a family in such health and love.

I remember one particular vacation, all together in Laguna Beach. One afternoon, I was videotaping my children playing in beautiful Shaw's Cove. And it all suddenly flooded back to me, right while I was filming:

That Laguna Beach chapter ... my last ditch effort at fighting off God's pursuit.

I could actually feel the pain of how hard I tried to prove I was someone worth loving. And now, transposed over those scenes, were my own children, occupying the exact same space. With the camera running, I started crying, and could not stop. ... In a box in our attic, is a five-minute clip of two-year-old Carly being knocked over by waves, laughing with her big brother, sister, and mom, while her dad is blubbering into the movie camera about God's redemption.

It all gradually caused me to want to offer this way of life to others. Most of my friends didn't grow up in families like this. I didn't grow up in a family like this.

As they got older and I watched them choose behaviors from trusting this life in Christ, I began to realize, "It works. This way of life in grace, it works!"

I wanted my family, our community of families, to be able to counter the prevailing theology that children brought up in grace would take advantage it, to live a double life.

I was watching a theory of grace become tested experience. It was astonishingly beautiful.

... And then it all seemed to unravel in a single phone call.

||||||||||||||||||||

Almost from the start, Amy's marriage had been hard. But I didn't know how hard. None of us did. Now, less than two years in, she was losing hope. We knew she was withdrawing. We just didn't know how to help. Her husband didn't want our counsel or help. So, we tried to give them room to work things out.

Amy is one of the finest humans I know. She is our kin-keeper. She is beautiful, thoughtful, and playful. She is funny and plays with people on their terms. Nobody has written more astoundingly undoing letters of affirmation to me.

That's partly why I was so devastated by the phone call.

Caleb calls, having just talked to Amy's husband. Stacey blurts out the "f" word. My wife has never used the word before. I think in that moment, I go into a form of shock. I innately know, whatever was just said, would change our family forever. Something precious has just fallen from my hands and shattered onto the floor.

Stacey gets hold of Amy. She tells her she's been hiding from us her involvement in a wrong relationship with another man. For some time.

"What! What does that mean? Who, when, uh, let me talk to her."

"She has hung up. She doesn't walk to talk right now. She wants to be alone."

"But, but, I'm her dad. I have to talk to her."

I dial her phone number twenty times in five minutes.

That night I lie in bed, churning and playing over and over questions that have no answers:

What do I do now? God, help me. What do I say to her? How did this happen? Oh God. I feel like I can't breathe. How do I protect Amy? How do I let her know I love her while I'm still trying to figure out how she got to this place? Should I call her husband? He doesn't want to hear from me. But I should call him. Help me God. Why wouldn't she want to talk to me? I've been through everything with her. Should I get in the car and drive out to California?

The damage is too devastating. Their marriage ends months later.

Amy comes back home from California. Our community swings into action to love her. She begins to face what happened. She is incredibly heroic. She went to college full of innocence and hope. Now she is trying to unravel what happened so quickly. She is bravely asking all the hard questions. She is facing what went wrong, especially her part in it. She is staying in the arena when it would be very easy to leave all who know her and land somewhere else where she could start over.

Amy is not a rebellious, immoral woman, acting out an immoral life. She is a godly woman, left vulnerable and ignoring the protection of those who love her, making frightened and exceedingly wrong choices.

Awakening: *All of us, left vulnerable by choosing to ignore protection, are fully capable of shocking and uncharacteristic wrong.*

I was convinced of this about my daughter from the moment I received the news. It has never wavered.

||||||||||||||||||||||

…... But still, I remained in shock.
Over the next months, I am emotionally and spiritually stuck.

> *How could this happen? I'm her father and her pastor. And somehow my own precious daughter chose to hide from us. Why did I not ask the right questions? Why didn't I see it? Why didn't I force my way in when I could see things weren't going well? How could I not know my own daughter was in distress, in a dark place? …*

If our family has three values, one of them would be that we wouldn't need to hide. I think almost every day of their growing up I spoke these words to at least one of my kids:

"Did anything happen today that hurt your heart? Is anything scaring you. Is there anything you're not sure how to tell us? The only thing we can't protect you from is what we don't know."

Both Stacey and I have been pretty transparent about our failures, individually and together. If we had a fight, we made sure afterwards to assure the children of our love and deep commitment. We told them what the argument was about and prayed God's protection for all of us. Because I lived the destruction of playing a double life with my own parents, I asked God that such would never exist in my home.

> *Why did this way of life I preach not work for my own daughter when she most needed it?*

On top of that, I'm devastated in believing that my family would no longer be able to represent this life in the way I thought we would.

How ridiculous! I was teaching grace everywhere, but I could not give the same grace now to myself. I did not yet understand the test of grace is not in keeping from failure, but in redeeming failure. Everyone will fail, under any view of God. How we treat each other when we do and how we find our lives again—this is where grace shines most brightly.

… It will take me quite awhile to understand those words.

Awakening: I cannot protect my children in the subjectivity of my shame but only in the objectivity of trusting my God with me … and them.

I begin to experience the physiological symptoms of someone in shock. I develop this shaky, shuddering sensation in my shoulders and back. A chronic, anxious weakness, which leaves me sometimes unable to draw a full breath. My words come out clumsily, with too much effort. This condition will stay with me, undiagnosed, for the next two years.

I am still on the road in the following months, speaking often. But my shame is hissing at me that I'm not fit to carry this message. Suddenly, I feel very much my age, and fifteen years more. I've lost confidence. I wonder if I'll ever return to full strength.

I'm still trapped, months and months after that phone call. God will slowly have to untangle the lie I carry. It says this should never have happened in a family that has believed these truths of grace so intentionally.

But he will show me that my understanding of grace does not make me or my children impervious to failure. No matter what I believe, each of my children have their own relationship with God, finding their own way, in their own choices. I do not have control over that.

Awakening: *It's a mistake to make myself responsible for the choices of anyone else, even my own children.*

This will be the last lie to be exposed.

Meanwhile, I am asking, "God, are you enough, now?" Some never get the freedom to risk asking it. **"The third part of my life I spent trying to convince myself the love I had found was enough."**

I write this in the middle of my darkest hours …

Jesus, they say you were tempted in all ways, like other men. I know it's true. But you can't have experienced the particulars of my generational distortion and twisted understanding.

How can you enter in, tonight, with me, into this madness? I know you love me in all of it, that you enter fully into the pain of my suffering and grieving. I know you suffered more than I will ever understand. But can you really relate to the suffering of my failure and regret? Can you know what it feels like to be as torn up as me? How can a sinless God fully empathize with a human who still carries sin?

So I lie in bed tonight, afraid, alone, feeling unknown. It is irrationally flooding me, all at once; I've claimed trusting my identity solves much of this, but it has not been solved in me.

I am a bluffer who writes books on authenticity. I am sad my kids are at an age where they don't seem to need me as their pastor and protector. It makes me feel useless—like my best days over. I fear my weakness makes me unattractive to my wife. I'm a controller. I use my fragility to avoid hard issues. I used to think I had the best friends in the world. Where are they now? What do I do that makes them leave? I lie about not wanting to be great. I spiritualize it into "having greater influence." I believe my issues would be solved if I was famous enough. I hate that I still carry that. I have held up my children as being nearly impervious to hiding. Now I feel foolish. I feel ashamed that my family now has a stigma attached to it. I get angry that I can't rally myself to again be the playful man of grace. I used to think my understanding of life made me immune to the regret of life others carry. But tonight, regret is all I carry. Tonight, all of my demons are out. I have never felt so alone. Can you stand to be with me in this ugliness, or have I run you off also?

…Then I remember. And at least for this night, I am safe.

You became my sin. You drank every moment of it to the dregs. You bore my shame. Not only bore it, you have drawn closer to me, loved me more profoundly, and covered me even more in this mess, than ever before.

Tonight does not define me. It is real. I will experience it again. But I am never alone in it … Once again, I sigh and whisper out into the dark … how did you find me here?

… and this:

"So, the other night as we are drifting off to sleep, I ask, 'Stacey, do you love me?' She answers, 'Yes, I do. More than ever.' I ask, 'More than ever? Why?' She answers, '… Because you need me more than ever.' And in the dark, I smile, sigh and fall fast asleep."

2012

Today I'm flying to Indianapolis. I'm returning four years later to a conference where I had one of the most profound speaking experiences of my life. That weekend, I was on my game and sharp and funny and apparently profound.

I will speak tonight and tomorrow night. I feel like crap. Whatever I have, it draws me inward and makes me want to be left alone. I'm tentative to talk much, because I can't get the words out as easily, in the short bursts this anxious constriction is allowing. I sound confused, frail, and less intelligent.

I've mispacked for this conference. I've been asked to dress "business casual." I don't possess this particular look. I have "casual" and "slovenly" but not business casual. I've brought a pair of corduroys, but I now discover they are hopelessly wrinkled. I try them on. I look like I've slept in them, several hundred times, on a rock quarry. I try to iron them, but it makes them look worse. Now they look rumpled and starched. I have no choice. I walk out the door, looking like Rip Van Winkle heading out on a blind date.

Before the main session, I've been asked to meet with a group who've been going through our book *The Cure*. I'm not up to this. I can speak to a large group and bluff my way through, but in a small group, answering questions and such, I'm a sitting duck. They'll see right through me.

I sigh, take a deep breath and whisper to God, "Help me. I'm all cold and locked up. I don't want to fail. I don't want to let these people down. I don't want to let Truefaced down. I don't want to let you down. I feel like I'm bluffing to be someone I used to be. I can't find myself right now. Help."

I walk into the room the group has reserved. Fifty or so are seated. I assume they're waiting for me to say something insightful or wise. I have neither.

So I start talking, trying to teach something, about something. Until I am stopped, midbluff.

One of them stands and says these words:

"John, we have something for you. For you, Bruce, and Bill. For your board, your staff, and anyone else who has ever helped you stand in this gap until this Original Good News found us. Would you give us the opportunity to each tell you how our lives are changed?"

For the next hour, one by one, they stand up and thank God for us, telling their own personal story of redemption. They are sobbing. Now I'm sobbing. I'm being given the gift of love from people I'd not previously known existed.

When they finish I stand up. "I did not want to come here tonight. I'm not doing well. I did not have anything much to give you." I give them a five-minute version of the last year and a half.

Without a word spoken, they all walk up to me and put their hands on my shoulders. They pray over me. That life-altering experience where you know you're not going through the motions, but actually believing God is present and powerful, doing something in this very moment. This meeting before this night's main session is a mightily important turning point for me.

John, I knew this hard and ugly time was going to hit you. So, I prepared this group to speak for me tonight. I knew you would need it exactly now. Believe every word. I have been doing this through you behind the scenes. I thought tonight you should see a sample of it.

Don't think you have been disqualified or diminished because of what has happened this last year. No. This is your moment of validation. You are getting to test out if this way of life in grace holds when the unthinkable gets thought. Millions need to know you still believe it, teach it, and risk living it, even when you are shaky and without full breath.

Now, you're about to walk into the main session to speak. You look terrible. Your pants are wrinkled. You have a facial tic thing going. You will struggle to find your words. At several points, you'll get lost in your notes. ... For you have lost a step, or three. Fear not. In such weakness, if you let me, I show up very strong. I've got this.

All right, tie your shoe. I don't need you falling off the stage. ... Be John Lynch. I'll be God. We work best this way.

2012

I'm holding the bread, taking communion this morning. I involuntarily asked myself, "Could I leave this? Could I do without this God, this faith, this life, all that has come to my soul with Jesus?" I'm asking the horribly scary question I might usually avoid, but now desperately needed to know my answer. Quickly, this came back: "Without Jesus, I can't make sense of anything. Forget heaven for a moment. Nothing today could hold my interest long, nothing could push back the absurdity and stop the emptiness if he is not real and near. Thirty years ago, there were so many other things I could have devoted myself to and fought valiantly for. I now have a life beyond anything I ever imagined. But without Jesus, none of it will hold me. He is the only meaning giving value to every other relationship, and why I'd dare to get out of bed and face the horrible things I know may come to me."

So I take the bread and then the cup. I not only have nowhere else to go. I cannot face the rest of this day without his love, his life, his intimate knowledge of me, his risking to carry my name and give me his. I'll stay in his love … or I'd perish. Besides, he paid too much. It's not up for grabs.

2012

Today, sitting down to prepare a sermon, I instead find myself writing this:

John, I know you are not on your game these days. You have not been for some time now. I know you long with all your heart to be on your game. You have begged me to get back to the clarity and strength of your past. I want you to know I probably will not be honoring that request. I do not say this with flippant indifference. This setback has given you a gift greater than you can yet know. You can hear. That's right. You're beginning to hear better. The pain, this lonely new longing, this shocking new shift inside you. It is waking up your heart. You are no longer feeling much in control. I hurt with you in the grief of what is no more. But I do not grieve over who you are maturing into. I do not need you to be on your game to have your life count magnificently. You will soon discover this is your most significant hour. I'm right here. I'm not playing you. This is not the result of your failure. By now, you must know better. I have taken the confusing loss this world has fashioned against you and I am turning it into the most significant hour of your life. You called to me the other night in a way we'd never yet shared. It overwhelmed me. Yes, me. Would not the one who is fully love experience the fullest response to love? You are receiving my love these days. You are returning love. It is raw, unvarnished and sputtering. But it is stunningly clear. Don't be afraid. You are not vanishing. You are not losing your mind. You are not losing your life. You are gaining it. I'm holding you together. This is what love ultimately longs to do. To be allowed to hold another together on this earth. Thank you, my friend.

2012

At first I wasn't sure. But yesterday I'm pretty certain I caught her glance as she was passing by. Noticing my eyes following her, she stopped and turned. We stared at each other, for nearly a minute. Then she smiled, as if in on a story and a series of events only she and I could fully appreciate. "Worry not, my friend. I'm not leaving. I'm circling back around for effect and a dramatic entrance. I'm here now. This current darkness is about to lift." I asked for her name. She said, "I wanted to be Joy. But it was already taken. My name is Hope." I involuntarily choked up as I barely got out these words: "I've missed you ... more than you can know." She smiled again, kindly speaking directly into my eyes. "I doubt it. ... Now, cut the chitchat. I've got a dramatic entrance to make."

... Thank you Father. Thank You for hearing my complaint, my honest pain and never imagining to hold it against me. Yesterday on the plane was the first time I've done that in years. This is all your doing. I almost never complain to you. All along you've been waiting for me to get it out. It's what friends do. I'm sorry I've been pretending like I wasn't disappointed. I was. You knew. You know me perfectly. And you knew it was all part of this particular ride. You are more stunning and real than I have ever known. Please keep renewing my heart. I am worth little to others without my passion and playful hope. Oh, she stopped and talked to me yesterday.

Hope. You caused that. Thank you, my stunning God. Thank you.

Love,
John

2013

My wife and I are sitting by the fireplace tonight. We sit out here a lot. Our children are no longer in our home. Carly is studying at Azusa Pacific University. Caleb and Amy both live nearby, here in Phoenix. Caleb and his wife Kali now have two children of their own. We have family dinners every Monday evening on this patio.

This evening, it's just us two. And a kale salad. She makes a killer kale salad! Black kale, lots of fresh garlic and lemon. You wish you knew someone who could make this salad.

Strands of lights hang above us. I am taking in this entire patio. All of it—this entire adobe and cobalt-tiled center, with fireplace, barbecue, and gas lamp—was a surprise and a gift. Ten years ago, some of our best friends, built all this on the weekend we were away for my fiftieth birthday. ... It has been the backdrop for so many of our celebrations, graduations and best times with family and friends.

Forks are scraping plates, while the crackle of cheap alley wood plays in the background. I love this particular combination of sounds.

I sigh.

It's a noticeably different sigh tonight. Wonderfully different than the sighs of the last two years. It is the sigh of contentment. "God. You've done it. You've been God to this family. You are protecting us. You are redeeming this chaos. We're still intact."

Over this last year, Stacey and I are enjoying our marriage like never before.

Awakening: *When crisis hits long and hard enough, we are all forced to decide whether we will blame each other or more deeply need each other.*

By the absolute grace of God, we have learned to need each other more deeply. Stacey is recuperating from uterine cancer surgery. The cancer turned out to be relatively noninvasive. But there is nothing routine about the time between being told something is very wrong and hearing the diagnosis. And there is nothing noninvasive about the robotic surgery which removed her uterus. But she faced it with such serenity, dignity, and trust in God. It has made her even more attractive and beautiful to my very soul. I'm in such awe of my wife. She has faced so much and yet is more mature, fun, and safe than ever before. She has allowed me to be strong for her.

She has also learned to allow me to be needy. In the past she has resented anything needy about me. No more. She has embraced my need. She is not afraid of my frailness. She has become my safest place. And something about her protection is making me more confident and strong.

God saw this coming all along. I have always loved Stacey. But there were times where I wanted to slip off to Burma and sell pamphlets on a street corner. I suspect there have been times where she wanted to club me in my sleep, wrap me up in carpet, tie it off with duct tape, drive me into the desert, and leave me for dead.

This love, I think, is born of dependence. I'm not sure I have always allowed my heart to need her. I'm not sure I knew how to let her in to protect me. She absolutely altered her life and dreams once she knew I needed her.

… She glances over at me, noticing my sigh. She can tell it's different. After twenty-nine years she can tell a change in sighs. It's quiet for awhile. She is trying to gather the words which have been forming for some time. Sitting together under the same blanket, both of us staring into the fire, she says,

"You don't see it, do you? You are the last to see the magic he is accomplishing in you." "What do you mean?"

"I love you so much, John Lynch. You don't see who you are, do you? You don't see what God's revealing. You are missing what has been taking place in you. You've been all bummed out, like it will always be hard. You can't see what we all see. So, let me tell you what I see. This last year has revealed you in magnificence, my husband. You are more kind to me. You don't power up. You don't make me feel judged. At least not as often. You're listening to my heart. You're more tender towards God. I am more at peace because of it. You are less opinionated, with fewer critiques you'll go to the wall for. God has done all this while you thought you were only holding on. I would never think I'd thank him for this last hurricane season of sadness. But tonight, with all my heart, I am."

I sigh again.

Several weeks from now, during a manuscript-editing meeting, Bruce will say, "I don't think you're telling the whole truth near the end of the book. I know a different John Lynch than what you're describing here. It is showing up all over the place. John, there is now more integration between what you teach and who you are. You are more mature, John. You're learning to trust his faithfulness on the windy, rocky slope. You no longer demand him to prove himself as good over and over by seeing resolve in every moment. And you also know this is not the last storm which will hit. But you are not nearly so afraid, confident he will be as faithful then as he has been before. You are now becoming that kind of mature.

"Your messages are more nuanced with insight. You are safer, kinder. You are wiser. You are not making yourself the issue when you describe a problem you see. We all see it. You are letting us in more. You are not going it alone in your weaknesses.

"John, you must tell this reality also. Or what good is God on your worst day? For if he doesn't use that difficult period to increasingly reveal the best John Lynch, then God makes little difference in this life. We should probably instead learn to cover up better. But he has done astounding things."

This too is why we need each other. To tell each other the truth we are often the last to see. I wanted this book to be an honest portrayal of real life. But I'm now realizing I haven't shown you the real truth unless I'm willing to articulate the incomprehensible redemption he is revealing. I guess I didn't want to write a happy-ending book, because not everyone's endings are clearly revealed as happy. But to miss this redemption would be to miss what God is doing in all of our stories. He will not waste pain. He will not waste suffering or hardship. He does the miraculous in us, in the midst and through such sections of our lives. This is actually what this book is all about!

Awakening: *It's not only how God sees me on my worst day, but what he does in me through my worst day that reveals the true nature of Christ in me.*

… It has happened. It is happening this evening. It will mark me for the rest of this ride. **"This fourth part of my life I am actually beginning to experience the life love has given me."**

2013

(Forgive me. I am list writer. I could not adequately express, only in story, what God taught me in my period of great darkness … my worst day. All of these, I imagine, could be considered "awakenings." Thank you for indulging me.)

Awakening: *For faith to avail, it usually must first appear as though it might not.*

- Christ's love holds even more fiercely in the storm.
- A tested grace is superior to an idealized grace.
- Fragile but authentic trust is more enjoyable to God than strong inborn capacity.
- I let go of some expectations of God while forming new and more significant ones.
- Love is experienced most when it is needed most.
- The best life is not the one with the least pain or suffering.
- God goes on doing his beauty when I opt out of trusting him. It's just that I miss it.
- The enjoyment of friends is more sacred when I rediscover them in my need.
- Jesus does not change in my darkest times. He remains a playful and true romantic.
- Jesus is enough…and he cannot and will not ever be taken from me.
- Laughter in a hard season is like stumbling upon a great red wine in a bus-stop cafeteria.

2013

These days my life is marked by one singular block directly outside my home. The place where God meets me—where I most accurately reflect on where I've been and where I'm going—is no longer in a pulpit, on the road, or in words typed onto an electronic page. Every time her parents bring her over, my nearly two-year-old granddaughter Maci points to the front door and urgently pleads these words to me: "Alk. Bawi, Apa." I choose to believe she is saying, "Walk. Bali. Pops." Bali is my dog. Pops is me. The walk is the two-hundred-yard stretch down to the corner and back. I used to carry her. She now loves walking nearly the entire route. I used to run four hundred yards in fifty seconds. It takes the three of us now over twenty minutes. They are the most sacred minutes of my week. Shuffling along, looking at details of a journey I rarely before noticed. This is all new to me. I've been slowly learning for it to be enough. On this stretch, I am Maci's safety net, allowing her to explore her new world. She is becoming my safety net to reexamine this world I stopped exploring awhile back. I kiss her and tell her I love her. She whispers back with a tender, trusting smile, "Yeah." In that moment, moments past sunset, shuffling along, with two creatures who think I'm one of the greatest humans alive, God surrounds the event. I'm almost sure he's saying,

I have not forgotten. Someday, you will shuffle this walk with someone taking your hand. Today, we are walking this walk, because holding her hand is healing you. All, so you can go back out and run, in health. Take your time. I'm in no hurry. I know what's up ahead. 'Tis all grace, my friend. Now, stop daydreaming. She's out in the street again. You might not want to let her put that cat poop in her mouth.

I look back. She is wearing a diaper and no shoes. We must be a sight to anyone passing by—a senile old man mindlessly wandering ahead of a child he can no longer find or dress. I scoop her up and carry her for a bit. In this moment, I am the happiest I've been in a very long time.

2013

Bruce McNicol once said, after a long, sometimes adversarial road trip, "It's like we're standing on a street corner, holding up rocket fuel in plastic bags, calling out, 'This stuff is crazy powerful! It'll change everything. … Now excuse me for a moment. These bags are leaking.'"

For much of the last twenty years, I've been part of this ministry movement named Truefaced. Bill and Bruce started it. But they are only some of the most recent voices who've been calling out since Day One. We've been trying to figure out how to help others discover this magical freedom of the Original Good News. What was, for moments, the only Christian voice on the market has now fallen upon hard times and is no longer the majority voice in the Body of Christ. We have stood often on street corners, rocket fuel leaking all over our pants.

There are days when I want to say, "Okay, Judiazers, you win. Live in your damned duplicity and corrupted sham! Poison the next generation, and the next. Knock yourselves out." I have tried to walk away and show up somewhere to preach polite messages the majority would enjoy. But it's like convincing myself to give up my love for Cockburn's music in favor of *The Greatest Hits of Carrot Top*.

(Again, here I go with the lists. But I thought you must see some of the tenets which have informed and animated my life. This way of life is starting to happen more and more. But the majority voice out there is still missing it. Here, I give the hope of grace and the damage where it does not exist.)

I dream in color of the Church one day:

- drawing out each other's new natures, instead of comparing behaviors.
- moving closer to each other when we fail.
- gaining permission to protect each other.
- creating environments of grace where there is safety to not hide.
- enjoying the intimate and unguarded closeness of a God who is already pleased with us.
- reaching to others with a gospel of hope for today, not only a remedy for heaven.
- living with heartfelt obedience instead of religious compliance.
- giving our life away as a response of love not as an effort to assuage our shame.
- breaking the "ought code" that is anesthetizing our kids from intimacy with Jesus.
- taking the moralistic filter off of God's Word, so it no longer condemns us.
- believing we're adored on our worst day, so we are free to take off the mask.
- resting in the absolute reality that a shame free story has been purchased for us.

Until that shift, our churches will continue to:

- try to change people who are already completely changed.
- measure our righteousness by how little we sin.
- withhold love from others because we're too busy earning love.
- believe knowing what is right is the same as the power to do right.
- be goaded to figure out how to please God, when he is already fully pleased.
- fail to protect each other, afraid, behind our fears of rejection.
- equate masculinity with machismo, thinking this will break our passivity.
- create more systems, techniques, programs, and methodology, thinking it will give us Jesus.
- beat ourselves up thinking, somehow, we will finally arrive at being enough.
- convince ourselves he is out there, over there, and up there instead of in here.
- not believe we are righteous, but instead live like saved, disappointing sinners.
- still think the correct slogan is "it's not about me." How ridiculous. It's about him in us.

Soon, very soon, the bags will no longer leak. And you will not be giving this out on street corners. It may not be you who get to see this, but it will happen before I return. This is my message. It is my responsibility. Your part is to keep trying new ways to get behind the lines.

2013

Late last afternoon Stacey and I opened a bottle of wine to sit out front and watch the sky change colors. The back of the bottle bears this description: "This blend presents aromas of

fresh mixed red berries, juicy cherries, and hints of vanilla ... that linger with red fruit notes through a long, smooth finish. ... Enjoy this wine with salads, pasta, and meats."

If there were any truth in advertising the label would read: "This bottle of swill is harsh and undesirable at first and then subtly changes into what kelp, vinegar, resin, and burlap might taste like if allowed to age between the nubs of a moldy shower mat. Enjoy this wine with food that starts with the letter x."

2013

Several weeks ago Bill said to me, "John, I was watching a special about Johnny Carson on PBS. All I could do was think about you. Johnny was an entertainer. You're an entertainer. You know that, right?"

I wanted to respond, "No! I'm a legitimate preacher guy, a writer, an articulator of profound things." Before I could answer, he said, "John, do have any idea how much our lives have been changed because you are an entertainer? Yes, you are owned by these truths as much as any of us. But you live them out as an entertainer!"

I sat there in my living room and let his words wash over me. I had never given myself permission to believe being an entertainer was godly enough. It is. It's how I have been fashioned by the God who loves me more than ten million yet unnamed galaxies.

2013

Nadine Houston and my wife pull a masterful surprise on their husbands. Doug and I discover on the way to our respective airports that we are going to meet together in Las Vegas.

The Houston and Lynch families have become lifelong friends these last few years. Doug and Nadine have been wonderfully transformed by these truths of grace since hearing a recording of a talk I gave years ago called "The Two Roads." Doug's now on the board of Truefaced.

Doug has recently been working incredibly hard, under intense pressure, in his businesses. The women decide what he needs most is to wander around Las Vegas.

With me!

… Sweet mother of creamed corn!

For three days, the four of us dine at some world-class restaurants. We buy really cool shoes at a store Stacey and I normally only walk past on dates. Doug and I are treated to an hour-long shaving experience, wearing hot face towels scented with something smelling like lemon cream pie. The four of us stroll the Strip and spend the entire evening at a prestigious steak house overlooking the Bellagio water show. We drink scotch that famous generals never got to taste. We stay up late and then sleep in as long as we want in fancy hotel rooms with those heavy, pitch-black curtains, electronically closing on their own. We are playing like dressed-up kids, driving a showroom Mustang convertible, cruising down Main Street on a warm Saturday night.

Nadine has also booked us to see a Garth Brooks concert.

I'm not a huge country western fan, but she has heard he puts on a fantastic show. If they want to see Garth Brooks, then so do we.

Just minutes before the show begins Nadine and Doug have to leave. Nadine is allergic to crab. She ate some at dinner, disguised as langostino, less than an hour ago. We are deeply sad for them, and a little sad for us. Stacey and I are now sitting next to each other, at a concert we might not have ever chosen.

What follows is one of my favorite three-hour blocks of time I've had in my life.

There is no band, no pyrotechnics. It's Garth, a single spotlight, and his guitar, in a relatively small room. He has put together an evening to honor all of the musical influences who have helped form his music. He is brilliant, winsome, anecdotal, funny, heartbreaking, heartwarming, and deeply inspiring. For three hours he keeps spellbound a beer-drinking audience with black hats and boots, expecting a night of rowdy country western. Instead they are getting artistry and life and hope. Cynical intellectual hipsters would be deeply moved. We are watching the culmination of a man's journey. He is brilliantly and naturally walking us through the life-shaping moments that came from hearing songs in his room on transistor radios and the radio dial of his father's car. After each song, he bows and gives the name of the artist he's been lauding. It's profound, nostalgic and immensely entertaining. We are riveted in our chairs. He's walking us through our own experience of the last decades. He's helping us interpret our own timelines. It is hard to say these words; but that evening may have been one of the finest shows I've ever seen.

But much, much more is happening for me this evening. As we slowly move with the crowd leaving the theater, my wife turns to me.

"I only know of two people in the world who have that kind of passion and storytelling ability to pull off such an evening.

"I'm standing next to one of them.

"John, forgive me for whenever I have devalued your gift and not supported to help promote it out of you for others."

I am dazed. We shuffle along with the exiting crowd, in silence. I am smiling, rocked by my wife's intimate knowledge of who I long to be at my core.

… God speaks to my heart in the moment.

Don't miss this John. I arranged for you to see this tonight. Worry not for Doug and Nadine. They will be cheering what I did for you. Besides, I am soon taking them on a cruise with their family that will cause them to momentarily forget your name. We are far from done with this journey. You are healing, maturing, coming alive, becoming free. You no longer carry the heavy bags that kept you from giving your version of the evening you just watched. You saw your future this evening. Listen to Stacey. Dream big, my friend. Dream with your heroes. Tell them what I'm telling you. They will know what to do with it. Tell them you're ready. Tell them you're not afraid. Then tell them you're very afraid. Tell them you're fully alive. Tell them you still have one long ride left in you. I have so many to reach, whose hearts will be opened only by story and self-effacing humor. What you learned in a VW doing all-night talk shows; what you learned on the stage for Dr. Witt; what you have learned telling stories in messages, I am now going to release. I've been doing it all along, but this may actually become your finest hour. Go figure.

Well, that's all I can tell you right now. This whole thing is still run by trust, not pre-information.

Kid, this is some of the payoff of your worst days. I never stop working in you. I never stop seeing the big picture. I never stop protecting what I put on your heart all those years ago. Sleep well, my friend. You're going to need it.

2013

I am listening to *The Good America* by Keith Jarrett this evening, sitting outside on the patio with my dog. I've got my ear buds in. Stacey's at a baby shower. Inside, thieves could be riffling through our refrigerator, filling their satchels with yogurt and cilantro. Out here, life is very, very good. Pillage away thieves, pillage away. Just don't come out to the patio and disturb me. My wallet is on the dresser. Leave me alone to my evening with my God. ...

2013

So, you're about to turn this manuscript in to the editors. If you don't mind, I'd like to offer several concluding remarks. This is not the end of our journey, but it is the last entry your readers will receive.

First, I know this is not the book you had originally hoped to write. Three years ago, you thought you could change the world by giving a picture of how grace could be lived out. You were strong and pretty assured of these truths.

Now that ship has sailed. Many of those you started this voyage with are no longer here. You are no longer strong. You can no longer hold the ropes as tightly. You are no longer as funny, clever, or full of capacity. Some of that capacity will never return in full measure.

I have spoken to you in the dark, before you even knew me, if only to give you the deep imprint of my love. Now I speak plainly, in the light.

You are living some of your finest moments on this earth. I know it doesn't feel that way. I know you had hoped for more—for smoother, for more influential, for easier. It's the nature of life on earth, that humans can't see what I'm doing in them. It's what makes evenings in heaven so special.

For these last thirty years you've asked me, "Am I teaching this correctly? Am I teaching something I only wish was true? Are you the way I've been telling others? I can do anything as long as I know I'm representing you in a way that glorifies you."

John, you have taught about me—my grace, how identity is lived out—all of it in great honesty and beauty. I think you've captured my voice exceptionally well. You used to hear me as never satisfied, always mildly disgusted, ready to expose and break you, presuming it must be for your own good. But you've come to believe how I see you, even on your worst day. Many never get this.

When you make up songs to me and sing them on long walks, I stop and turn, closing my eyes until you're done. I miss nothing, but I draw even closer at such times. You need never doubt the depths of my affection and care. I could not be more happy with our relationship. You need not try to pray more, read more, do anything more. Respond to this new life in you. Your affections are wired for me. When you're thirsty, drink.

Life will not necessarily get much easier. But it will get richer. You will read books to children more. You will drink wine with your wife more. You will understand even more fully why I gave her to you. You will see me resolve relationships you thought were forever broken.

John, you will need, more than ever, to allow others near you. Let them tell you the truth of what they see. They are your fans. They have much invested in your health and joy. You used to say, "No one can know this is true about me." Now you are learning to say, "I must be certain that the people I trust know the absolute truth about me."

Oh, and you will go back to Dodger stadium. You'll take grandchildren. You will buy them malts with those wooden spoons. You will buy them Dodger Dogs and bobble-head dolls. You will purchase upper deck seating because it is still what you can afford.

2013 Summer

We are here. "Here" is Puerto Penasco, Mexico. And "we" is my entire family—Stacey, John, Caleb, Kali, Amy, Carly and our grandchildren Maci and Payton. We are on vacation.

Amy and I are on the beach ... running.

That last phrase may mean little to you. To me, it carries more unbridled splendor than I have keystrokes to convey.

First, I am sixty. I have not "run" in over a decade. Yes, I've limped the old-man-survival-shuffle for blocks at a time. It is more of an extended controlled fall than a jog.

I ran a marathon once, when people could still watch a movie outdoors. From their car.

I damaged my legs badly back in the early '90s. I tried to run several miles back home one day on a badly strained calf. I've never been the same since. I went to a specialist about it, unwilling to give up running. He did a few tests and took some internal pictures. He deadpanned these words:

"John, when you think of your calf muscles, imagine strands of beef jerky, loosely tied to a bone on either end."

... Nice bedside manner, Doc.

But God has formed today's scene, from long before oceans and sand existed.

We start out so slowly. I am predicting my shuffle will be stopped by muscle tightness and shooting pain, as it usually does. But something about this setting, out on firm sand, with an ocean to my right and my daughter on my left, is different than usual.

... There is no pain. There is no limp. With each step, there is less caution.

I gradually pick up the pace. Amy and I are now breathing in unison, striding down the shore. I take off my shirt. I feel almost thirty-three again!

I am becoming quickly aware this is no longer a run. It is the revealing of God's vindicating and redemptive love and eternal intention.

I continue to stride out, faster and faster. "Faster" might be a nine-minute pace. But I have not felt this familiar feeling of well-earned exertion in so long! It would normally be very painful. Except I've missed it so much, I'm gulping it all in, with every breath.

Nearly two miles into the run, Amy looks over at me. She stares a long time. I can feel her gaze. I look back over at her. We are both beaming at each other, now nearly galloping.

I turn back, straight ahead, pushing forward even faster. She calls out, above the sound of the waves, this one word:

"Impressive."

We are locked into a moment of God's finest quality of appreciation. I am lost in the eternal, lost in how absolutely great he is.

I am lost in my love for my daughter, lost in my respect, admiration, and endless pride of who she is—maturing into a far more beautiful woman than the one I knew before the darkness. She is healing, coming full alive, fully herself, deeply in love with God.

She is opening again to me. It feels like that day when I opened her car door to discover all those note cards taped to her dash. Later this evening, she and I will opt out of the family trip into town. We will dress up and go on a date, strolling around this resort. We will continue to allow each other back into the deep places of trust and love.

I mouth this word back to her, with insufficient breath to make it audible: "Impressive."

I am lost in shattered gratitude.

As my body begins to seize up into near crisis, I am unwilling to allow this moment to end. God is revealing himself again, in such intensity, I momentarily wonder if I will suddenly have a heart attack and come home. He has been more to me than I ever imagined I had capacity to experience. I am ready. I push harder, happily forcing the issue for God.

And I say this word to him inside my head, breathing now in short gasps:

"Impressive."

Afterword

From Bill Thrall and Bruce McNicol

Congratulations on finishing an exhilarating adventure into the life of our esteemed friend and co-author buddy, John Lynch. Can you imagine working with this guy? Whoa. Piece of work. For us, it's part Melodrama, part Saturday Night at the Improv, and part stunning joy of Narnia. One day, we'll tell you the "rest of the story."

But, now, we are interested in your story. If you're like us, you long for your story to be true and to matter. Reading *Worst Day* probably only increased your longing for the freedom of a trusted and authentic community, where your story could be heard and could flourish. A place, which nurtures your healing, maturing, and best contributions in this life. We want you to experience such a life!

The three of us, along with our wives, our families, and our friends are part of a larger community anchored in committed relationships of trust. This community is far more important than any bestselling books we have authored, and exceedingly more significant than our greatest strategic plans. It is from this imperfect, yet authentic environment that we write. Experiencing the power of such community for decades now, inspires our relentless vision to see hundreds of thousands of similar high-trust, communities of grace multiplied around the world. That's the real mission of these books, to give you the hope of a life that for too long, and for too many, has seemed beyond reach.

So, if *Worst Day* captured your imagination for this way of life, we invite you to read or listen to another book, called *The Cure*. In The Cure, we take you on a journey down a road less traveled, leading to the fountainhead of these powerful communities, the God-principles. Think of it as *The Cure… for your worst day.*

To your story, by God's grace!

Bill Thrall & Bruce McNicol
Co-authors, with John Lynch, *The Cure, Bo's Café, Behind The Mask,*
Also, *The Ascent of a Leader, Beyond Your Best, High-Trust Cultures*

To access these resources, and for our Trust One Center online campus, please reach us at **www.truefaced.com**

Acknowledgments

For years I wanted to write a book on grace and the voice of God from a personal perspective. I imagined that it might help change the culture. When it came time to write it I couldn't easily change our trashcan liner.

But Bill Thrall and Bruce McNicol wouldn't let me believe my lies. Whatever I know about loving protection, much of it has come from these two men. Bruce had the courage to tell me my first effort was disproportionally dark, inaccurate and meandering. He kindly compelled me to write the truth of what God had done in me on my worst day. Bill, who rarely has any artistic insight, was forced to give me this book's creative layout. These two are much of the reason why this book exists and why I haven't run off with the circus and forfeited the influence of my life.

When I began the project, I knew the person I wanted to hear most from was my friend and immensely talented writer Bob Ryan. His first words were, "The only thing I know for sure is that the title of the book will be On My Worst Day." Thank you for your honesty and belief in me.

To Stacey. She believes in me so much...and could care less if I ever wrote a pamphlet. Somewhere in this process she allowed me to start reading snippets to her. At one point she said, "Hey wait, I like these! I would read these in a book. You should keep going...Read me another one." Oh, how I adore Stacey Marie.

My relationship with Crosssection has not been that of an author-publisher, but rather gifted publishing friends who are driven to reshape culture. Doug Martinez and Jason Pearson demand this message of the Original Good News be told as revolution. Doug's care for me and honesty forced him to call me one evening to tell me that the book cover I had chosen was fine but would miss a chance at revolution. Jason is a freak of nature. Much of his own artwork is astounding and shockingly controversial. But he has worked way beyond expectation to create the media exactly needed for this subtly subversive message. Kris Hull did much the same.

Every writer should have Jordan Green as their developmental editor. He mocks my writing and insults me at every turn. Then, in the next breath, he will tell me how he cried through the next piece. Linda Harris was my text editor. If there is any hint of the English language being honored in this book it is largely from her resplendent skills. John Pearson spends most of his time changing the world on boards, organizations and consultancy. Until we write a book. Then he humbly protects us in the last hour, catching typos and errors which would make us look like we wrote the manuscript buzzed on floor polish. He is one of the most vital friends of this message.

And to my village…

To Open Door. There has not been one moment in forty years where this rag-tag, family of absurdly failed and wonderfully vulnerable lovers has not dared to risk this word "grace." It is still magically felt by everyone who walks in your doors. You changed and continue to change the way I hear the voice of Jesus. Where would I be without this community?

To the board of Truefaced, our amazing staff and our Advisory Council. Your refusal to let this message fail has made you our heroes. You bring your capacities and sacrifice for free and make us feel like you're stealing to get to do it.

To my children: Caleb, Amy and Carly. You did not have a say in being brought into this grand experiment. You have never been pastor's kids. You have instead risked the very same truths your mom and dad did. You wanted this to be real as much as we have. And your lives prove its truth as they shine so bright-ly. I could not be more proud of each of you.

And to every friend I have all over this world, met and unmet, who have championed to risk goodness when everything around you looks chaotic. You have trusted the Original Good News on your worst day. And now we have found each other…and are discovering we were separated at birth.

It's almost like there's a God or something.
Rock on.
John Lynch

OTHER BOOKS FROM TRUEFACED

The Cure

What if God isn't who you think He is and neither are you?

The Cure gives the diagnosis of this century's religious obsession with sin-management. It has poisoned the Church, obscuring the Original Good News and sending millions away—wounded, angry and cynical, from nearly any organized expression of faith. The Cure offers an authentic experience in Christ that frees some from a self-rewarded righteousness, and others from a beaten down striving for a righteousness they can never seem to attain. The Cure infuses a relational theology of grace and identity, which alone can heal, free and create sustainable, genuine, loving, life-giving communities.

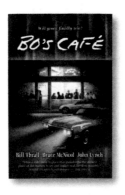

Bo's Cafe : A Novel

High-powered executive Steven Kerner is living the dream in southern California. But when his bottled pain ignites in anger one night, his wife kicks him out. Then an eccentric mystery man named Andy Monroe befriends Steven and begins unravelling his tightly wound world. Andy leads Steven through a series of frustrating and revealing encounters to repair his life through genuine friendship and the grace and love of a God who has been waiting for him to accept it. A story to challenge and encourage, Bo'S Café is a model for all who struggle with unresolved problems and a performance-based life. Those who desire a fuller, more authentic way of living will find this journey of healing a restorative exploration of God's unbridled grace.

Behind The Mask

Reversing the Process of Unresolved Life Issues

The act of sin—ours or someone else's—creates within us an involuntary response of either guilt or hurt, which leads to the inevitable effects of pain, turmoil, and mask wearing. Understanding how to reverse the process of unresolved life issues is what Behind the Mask is all about.

For more information on the Trust One Center online campus, please see www.truefaced.com

About the Author

As a great communicator and writer, John Lynch is a vital staff member of the Truefaced team and co-writer of bestsellers Bo's Cafe and The Cure.

Since 1997, John has been speaking nationally with the Truefaced team, often acting out the popular Two Roads message and delivering compelling talks of living out of new identity. He is currently also a co-designer and a primary faculty member in Truefaced's newly developed Trust One Center online campus and their Life Application Courses.

John served for twenty-seven years as teaching pastor at Open Door Fellowship in Phoenix, Arizona. The authenticity, longevity, and playfulness of these two flawed communities, Open Door and Truefaced, brings real-world validity and wide reaching application to this message of the Original Good News.

For fifteen years John co-founded and helped write, direct and act in Sharkey Productions, a Gospel-anchored theater group, eventually performing in the prestigious Herberger Theater.

It is nearly documented that few can eat food as fast, or hold their breath under water as long as John.

John and Stacey are enjoying their marriage more wonderfully than at any time of the last thirty years.

Their youngest, Carly, is the family's resident theologian, studying for her Masters of Divinity at Azusa Pacific University. Amy is the family kin-keeper and a dental hygienist, living in Phoenix. Caleb is a children's sports director, as well as a cross country and track coach at Arizona Christian University. He and his wife Kali have brought Maci and Payton into this unrehearsed and deeply loving family.